Not of This World

Religious Liberty for All

as a key Christian and American Value

Lemuel V. Sapian

NOT OF THIS WORLD :

Religious Liberty for All as a Key Christian and American Value

http://www.notofthisworldbook.com

For more information contact :

Brimingstone Press

5301 Alpha Rd, Suite 80 #200

Dallas, TX 75240

http://www.brimingstone.press

Book and Cover design by *Brimingstone Writer Services*

ISBN: 978-0-578-22797-9

First Edition: November 2019

1 2 3 4 5 6 7 8 9 10

Table of Contents

Dedication

To Shane, Matthew, Mark, and Amelia,
May you live in a world with freedom of conscience.
To Michelle,
Your love is an inspiration.
To Christ,
You are my everything.

INTRODUCTION

THE CONCEPT OF RELIGIOUS LIBERTY is a very hotly debated subject. With the tendency of religion to bleed into many different areas of politics, it is a subject that is hard to avoid because it involves the very convictions of men. Even for those that wish to remain agnostic and largely uninvolved with religion, it somehow finds some way to influence one aspect of life or another.

Because man's basic beliefs are an important part of his being, religion becomes a very sensitive topic for many. With this in mind, there is no doubt that no other religion has shaped the history of this planet more than Christianity. The primary Sacred Scriptures of Christianity, the Bible, is considered the most influential and best-selling book of all time.

American Christians are proud of their country's legacy. But as America continues to grow in population, her cultural, ethnic and religious makeup also grows in diversity. Conservative American Christians grow fearful that the national culture based upon what they perceive are Judeo-Christian values and ethics will be replaced by a secular ethos. This fear, exacerbated by recent actions of radical religious rivals such as Islam, has Western Christianity searching for a way to protect its identity and integrity.

This reactionary attitude is not new. In the mid-twentieth century, Western Christianity's main opponent was atheistic communism. The totalitarian despotic nature of the communists has been mirrored by the tyranny of radical Islamic terrorists today. These global examples of religious and anti-religious tyranny are just part of the many conflicts that span the globe since the beginning of time. Hindus have persecuted Muslims, and Buddhists have as well. Religious wars have been a staple of our historical existence on this Earth.

Some atheists and agnostics have tried to argue that religion is the primary cause of these devastating conflicts, but the historical experiment of anti-religious movements in suppressing religious thought and practice has also resulted in wanton violence and persecution, starting with the French Revolution's anticlerical "Reign of Terror" and continuing in the antireligious Socialist and Communist regimes of the twentieth century.

Amid the growing tensions and conflict between religious belief systems that used state actors to further their secular ambitions grew the Land of Liberty, the United States of America. Out from fledgling colonies that struggled with keeping the peace between bodies of different religious convictions came a united nation built on the ideology that the more civil government is separated from religion, the better for both. America's strength did not come from a forced religious conformity. It came out of the concept that there could be "unity in diversity", that the secular interests of the nation could still be safeguarded despite the diversity in personal religious belief.

This book is a study on how the Christian background of America has led to its character of religious toleration and freedom, and why the nation needs to keep this part of her heritage, even if it was to the perceived detriment of Christianity's theological claims in a growing sea of religious diversity.

While this book is addressed primarily to and concerns American Christians, adherents of all faiths and no faith can understand how the idea of religious tolerance came to be and what Christianity's relationship to this concept is. Muslims who read this volume will be able to gain an understanding of why many American Christians are vehemently against Sharia Law. Hindus and Buddhists who read this will have a greater understanding of proper Christian concepts of morality and civil law. Jews who read the book will understand how the New Covenant theology of Christianity contributes to the idea of a Church and State separation. Atheists who read this will realize how the maturity of Christianity encouraged the Enlightenment and gave rise to the civil concepts of religious liberty in America that they enjoy today.

The Christian who reads this book and who will search the Scriptures will see the plain Biblical reasoning for an abandonment of the ambition to gain temporal power, even if the intention was to "defend" the Christian faith and practice. God's Kingdom is "not of this world", and those that wish to be citizens of the Heavenly abode, while continuing to honor and respect their Earthly government, must set their eyes primarily on a nation which has no Earthly borders but whose realm includes the most infinite recesses of the cosmic universe.

For the un-earthly Kingdom of God,

Lemuel V. Sapian

James Madison, by John Vanderlyn, 1816

"We are teaching the world the great truth that Govts. do better without Kings & Nobles than with them. The merit will be doubled by the other lesson that Religion flourishes in greater purity, without than with the aid of Govt."

James Madison, *Letter to Edward Livingston*, July 10, 1822

Jesus Before Pilate, First Interview
(Jésus devant Pilate. Premier entretien)
by James Tissot, c. 1890

"Jesus answered, My kingdom is **not of this world**: if my kingdom were of this world, then would my servants fight, that I should not be delivered to the Jews: but now is my kingdom not from hence."

John 18:36, KJV

CHAPTER ONE

Historical Past-Retentive Syndrome

WE ROMANTICIZE THE STORY of the Pilgrim forefathers of our American nation. The tale of the Mayflower is a story our children love to hear, and generations upon generations of Americans tell their offspring. "America…is the land of opportunity and freedom," we tell our young ones. But has that always been the case? Have we been the bastion of liberty we often sing about in our classrooms, and the "One nation, under God" we often recite as a pledge to our flag?

Religion is a topic that garners much attention anywhere you go. It is an integral part of whole cultures and decides the progress or decline of civilizations. Nations are formed with religion often at the forefront of issues. Ethics and values are formed by religious views. It certainly isn't any different when it comes to the history of America.

There is no doubt that America is a Christian nation, however not by civil declaration or fiat, but by culture and influence. Although historically Protestant, America has recently seen the rapid decline of individuals identifying as such. [1]

Even with this decline, however, there is no question Americans owe a large part of their culture to Protestant Christianity. After all, the first European settlers to this continent were devout Puritans who splintered off of the Church of England.

When it comes to the Pilgrims aboard the Mayflower, we regale our guests and children with the story of how our

---

[1] Lipka, Michael. "10 Facts about Religion in America." *Pew Research Center*, 27 Aug. 2015, <**www.pewresearch.org/fact-tank/2015/08/27/10-facts-about-religion-in-america/**> Accessed 23 June 2019.

forefathers fled from religious oppression and persecution to settle in a land of freedom and opportunity.

If only the story were that simple. It is true that the Pilgrims, which were a sect of Puritans, did seek peaceful asylum from the growing religious and political intolerance in England. But they sojourned through the Netherlands first, finding the religious tolerance pioneered among the Dutch to be attractive. Fearing the loss of their cultural identity, however, they arranged to travel to the New World, with its allurement of adventure and a brand-new start.

The Pilgrims that formed the Plymouth Bay Colony learned from their experiences of being oppressed in England and adopted a certain level of religious tolerance. The Puritans which followed them and formed the Massachusetts Bay Colony were another story altogether. Suffice to say, they were not very religiously tolerant at all, which was not without its irony, given their struggles in the Old World.

The Massachusetts Puritans imposed strict religious laws intended to enforce their brand of Puritanism upon whoever would venture to dwell within their borders. This would otherwise be a fair agreement except for the fact that people of other religious backgrounds and beliefs began to pour into the colony to escape their plights.

The mixing of church and state isn't a Puritan invention.

The Anglicans which persecuted them, and which they sought refuge from in the New World, also mimicked the Roman Catholics who initiated military Crusades to try and wrest lands from the Muslims, and also used them to crush internal heretical movements.

All this interest in Christendom to acquire material wealth and political power is very intriguing. Especially given the fact that Jesus Christ sought not to establish a worldly kingdom, but instead a Kingdom not of this world; one that would never end. Thanks to human greed and lust, the mission of Christianity has become marred with the want of worldly gain.

But how did this happen? It happened because those that professed to be "Christians" departed from the simplicity of the Gospel of Jesus Christ and used worldly power and lust to control others. It is a sad tale of moving from being persecuted for Christ's sake to being the persecutors of others when they did not agree with their precepts.

A classic tale of "repaying evil for evil", the story of religious oppression by Christians upon non-Christians and fellow Christians begins when the Roman Empire moved from its Pagan roots to embracing Christianity as a political tool to consolidate power. Ironically enough, instead of strengthening the Empire, it actually signaled the beginning of its decline.

The moment Christianity became the state religion of the

Empire thanks to the Edict of Thessalonica in 380 AD, it became akin to a kingdom of this world. While it can be argued that Christianity was a positive influence in the spread of Western culture and civilization and was a welcome prospect for its time when many cultures were pagan and savage, the bringing in of the message of the Gospel to the world using worldly strategies and methods have caused damage to the image of Christianity in the eyes of many.

The Scriptures themselves state so unequivocally that we must not love the world or its concepts. Lust for power, and the human penchant for making others conform to their ideas using coercive methods is a worldly concept which we must shun:

> *"Love not the world, neither the things that are in the world. If any man love the world, the love of the Father is not in him."*[2]

The want of worldly power to advance ostensibly spiritual goals is exactly what Christ warned the Pharisees of His day about. During the age before the Renaissance (14th – 16th Century) and the Reformation (16th – 19th Century), a myriad of various doctrines, traditions, and customs permeated

---

[2] 1 John 2:15, *King James Version*

through the civilized world, dictating the politics of the day. It was one way the nobility of the Dark (5th – 10th Century) and Middle (10th – 14th Century) Ages were able to keep the commoners in-line and was also used as a weapon against political adversaries.

Excommunication, for example, was used to punish perceived offenders of Canon Law and heretics. It was supposed to be used for the severest of offenses and in the Middle Ages had the tendency to bring whole nations under extreme political pressure, especially when heads of state were excommunicated. However, it became a political, even civil tool used in some of the most trivial cases, such as when the Bishop of Lincoln, John Dalderby excommunicated several individuals for not disclosing the location of a missing nobleman's falcon in 1304.[3]

The mingling of church and state caused so much strife during the Dark and Middle Ages; it sparked various Crusades and Inquisitions that consigned individuals and groups to a death sentence by authorities and armies "devoted" to the cause of the Papacy and the Pope who is considered *Vicarius Christi,* or the Vicar of Christ.

---

[3] Hill, Rosalind. "The Theory and Practice of Excommunication in Medieval England", *History*, vol. 42, Issue 44, 1957.

To be fair, one could say the historical political power grab of Christianity was a reaction to the political suppression of Christianity in its early days. The persecution of early Christian believers by the Jewish establishment, the persecution of Christians by the Emperor Nero through the Emperor Diocletian certainly left a bitter pill in the mouth of the Christian establishment before the rise of religious toleration for them under the reign of Constantine the Great.

It also didn't help that the rapid rise of Islam in the 7th century stoked fires of a budding rivalry between the two rapidly growing Abrahamic religions, both seeking to defend their hegemony over their respective regions in the civilized world. With all these factors it isn't surprising that Christianity would emerge as a powerful political world player by the end of the first millennia AD.

But the fact that Christianity was persecuted in the past and had to compete with an alarmingly growing emergent Muslim threat is no justification for Christianity to develop similar traits to its persecutors. The very principles of Christianity prohibit it from being coercive and vindictive, and when applied properly, it results in more religious tolerance and freedom for others. As we will see later when we discuss the rise of the principles of liberty as we see in the American experience, Christianity plays a central role in the religious freedom experiment; however not in the way a lot of American Christians envision.

Christian Nationalism has supplanted the simple truths of the Gospel and has become enamored with worldly gain. We as believers in the Gospel of the Kingdom of Christ must shun all worldly attachments with a singular vision to make disciples of all nations, not just the one we are in. I believe America is blessed beyond measure, but only because she has embraced the principles of freedom and liberty and has become a haven for the oppressed and downcast of all races, cultural origins, and religious beliefs. The Bible tells us,

"Learn to do well; seek judgment, relieve the oppressed, judge the fatherless, plead for the widow."[4]

These principles of simple godliness we must follow, and as citizens of a Heavenly Nation eternal and glorious, we will find that Christ's Kingdom is not the United States of America; it is a Kingdom with no Earthly borders and includes individuals from all Earthly nations, tribes, tongues, and people.

This is why America is blessed by God; we have learned

---

[4] Isaiah 1:17, *King James Version*

to separate the civil from the divine. During the colonial era we saw huge Empires claim swathes of land in the name of their kings, Emperors and "God". Religion became a tool of oppression and a weapon of power. However, we also saw oppressed groups of God-fearing people seeking havens from persecution, and this drove many settlers to seek new parts of the world to settle.

The lands of the New World became the haven of persecuted groups of people, seeking only follow the dictates of their conscience and live in peace. But unfortunately, this attitude was not adopted by all, even among the early New World settlers and colonists. In the following chapters, we will be analyzing this phenomenon in pre-American history and how it shaped the governing principles of the American nation, and how it embodies the very precepts of Christianity itself down to its core.

The concept of Church and State separation in the interest of true and proper Religious Liberty is often a very misunderstood principle even among Christians. For Christians to apply it properly they must understand what Christ was saying when He was brought before civil authorities leading up to and right before His crucifixion. The Jewish establishment of His day sought a Messiah that would liberate Judea from the iron rule of the Roman Empire.

To understand Jewish apprehension further, we must look at their history. For centuries before the Roman rule, the Jews were kept as a client state, subjected to the authority of various Empires. The Biblical book of Daniel chapter 1 tells of the beginning of the Judean exile into the land of Babylonia. The book of Daniel also tells of how Babylon fell to the Medo-Persian Empire, and we know that after that the Persians gave way to the Hellenistic Empire during the conquests of Alexander the Great.[5]

Daniel tells of how the Babylonians gave a degree of religious freedom to the Jews, thanks to his and his close friends' involvement in the royal court. The Persians also gave a degree of liberty to the Jews during their rule, with a close call occurring when Haaman, the erstwhile henchman of the King attempted genocide against the Jews, thwarted only by Queen Esther's intervention. The Persians even allowed the Jews to return to their land and begin to rebuild their capital city.

It was during the rule of the Hellenistic kings that the Judeans began to feel more acutely the oppression of a Gentile government on their religious convictions, and this came to a head during the reign of Antiochus IV Epiphanes, the Seleucid

---

[5] The story is found in Daniel chapters 1-3.

king who issued a decree to ban Jewish rituals and practices. A brutal uprising followed, led by the Maccabee brothers, who later founded the Hasmonean dynasty.[6]

You would think the Jews would learn from the pain of religious oppression, all the way back from their days of slavery in Egypt, that they would treat others of similar plights with such understanding. Unfortunately, those that forget their history often repeat it, and in the case of many persecuted groups, they turn around and inflict the same horrors they experienced on others.

I would like to refer to this phenomenon as *Historical Post-Retentive Syndrome* (henceforth referred to as HPRS). Essentially what this refers to is the failure of later generations to retain the memory of bitter past experiences and lessons. In the study of the history of religious oppression there are too many examples of HPRS as group after group falls into a similar cycle of persecuting others after escaping their previous persecutors.

For example, Buddhists met harsh persecution in Communist countries and from Catholics in the South Vietnamese regime before its fall at the end of the Vietnam

---

6 Atkinson, Kenneth. "A History of the Hasmonean State: Josephus and Beyond", pg. 25.

War.[7] A little over three decades later the predominantly Muslim Rohingya faced ethnic cleansing by the predominantly Buddhist ultra-nationalist government of Myanmar.[8] Being a classic textbook example of HPRS at work, this sad series of events will result in perpetuating the continuing cycle of violence and persecution.

History is replete with examples of the pervasiveness of HPRS with every culture and group. The freedom of conscience is one of the most beleaguered principles in human society throughout history. Millions have died because of the mere idea of being free to believe in the transcendent, or not to believe. Freedom of conscience is a principle that affects all and cannot be used to apply to merely a privileged few.

This is the beauty of the American principle of Religious Liberty, where Church and State are by principle, separate[9],

---

[7] Adam Roberts, "Buddhism and Politics in South Vietnam", *The World Today*, Royal Institute of International Affairs, London, vol. 21, no. 6, June 1965, ppg. 240–250.

[8] Sapian, Lemuel V. "Rohingya refugees from Myanmar tell stories of genocide", *ReligiousLiberty.TV*, 10 April 2018.

<**http://religiousliberty.tv/rohingya-refugees-from-myanmar-tell-stories-of-genocide.html**> Accessed July 19 2019.

[9] Jefferson, Thomas. *"Letter to the Danbury Baptists."* Received by Nehemiah Dodge, Ephraim Robbins, & Stephen S. Nelson, 1 Jan. 1802.

and this line of thinking has its roots in the Enlightenment[10] and, before that, Protestant Christian[11] thought. Indeed, it is the core principles of Christianity as taught by Christ that formulate the very basis for Religious Liberty and toleration for all as civil principle.

In the next few chapters, we will be exploring why civil religious toleration should be a core tenet of the Christian belief system, and how America has succeeded and failed in adopting this core value throughout the years. I hope that this volume will serve as a reminder of the dangers of HPRS, and how we can avoid repeats of religion-driven violence and oppression in the future.

---

[10] Zafirovski, Milan (2010), *The Enlightenment and Its Effects on Modern Society*, p. 144

[11] Walker, Andrew T. "The Reformation and Religious Liberty: A Conscience Bound to Government or God?" *ERLC*, 4 July 2017,

<http://erlc.com/resource-library/articles/the-reformation-and-religious-liberty-a-conscience-bound-to-government-or-god> Accessed 20 June 2019.

CHAPTER TWO

Lessons from History

THE RHYTHMIC BEATING OF DRUMS pierced the morning Friday air on June 1, 1660. 49-year-old Mary Dyer marched solemnly, flanked by an armed escort, through the misty streets. The erstwhile Puritan turned Quaker was found guilty of violating a ban on Quakers living in the area. This ban was enforced by the pain of death.[12]

The gallows consisted of a large elm tree from which hung

---

[12] Rogers, Horatio (1896). *Mary Dyer of Rhode Island, the Quaker Martyr That Was Hanged on Boston Common*, June 1, 1660, ppg. 3-4.

a rope. Once she was brought to the site, she was allowed to give up her faith and thus save her from execution. Her response was direct and pointed:

"Nay, I came to keep bloodguiltiness from you, desiring you to repeal the unrighteous and unjust law of banishment upon pain of death, made against the innocent servants of the Lord, therefore my blood will be required at your hands who willfully do it; but for those that do is in the simplicity of their hearts, I do desire the Lord to forgive them. I came to do the will of my Father, and in obedience to his will I stand even to the death."[13]

Moments later the drums stopped, and Mary Dyer was swung from the rope and she died, a martyr for her beliefs. If one didn't know better, we'd have guessed she was martyred in the volatile politico-religious atmosphere of 17th century Europe. No, she was executed at the gallows on Boston Common, in the same Boston which was the center of the Massachusetts Bay Colony. The same Massachusetts Bay Colony that was supposed to be a haven for New England Puritans escaping Anglican persecution.

---

[13] Ibid., ppg. 60-61.

But as with many countless cases in history, HPRS rears its ugly head again and again. The cycle of religious oppression will continue with no end because we have failed to recognize the key to being treated with respect is to treat others with respect. It is the classic golden rule,

"And as ye would that men should do to you, do ye also to them likewise."[14]

This rule isn't found just in Christianity but in many other religious traditions around the world. The ethicist and author Rushworth Kidder identified this basic principle in many of the world's major religions, including Buddhism, Hinduism, Judaism, and Taoism.[15] Philosopher Simon Blackburn echoes Kidder's conclusions, noting that the Golden Rule exists in "some form in almost every ethical tradition".[16]

In Buddhism, for example, we find, "Hurt not others in ways that you yourself would find hurtful."[17] In Judaism we

---

[14] Luke 6:31, *King James Version*

[15] Kidder, Rushworth M. *How Good People Make Tough Choices: Resolving the Dilemmas of Ethical Living*, pg. 159.

[16] Blackburn, Simon (2001). *Ethics: A Very Short Introduction*. pg. 101

[17] *Udanavarga* 5:18

find,

"What is hateful to you, do not do to your fellow: this is the whole Torah; the rest is the explanation; go and learn."[18]

The ancient Greek rhetorician Isocrates (436-338 BC) taught, "Do not do to others that which angers you when they do it to you."[19] There are many instances that this maxim is repeated through many ethical traditions and religious belief systems.

How then, is it possible that this maxim, this "Golden Rule" is not commonly practiced? It is because in many believers, especially in those who are granted the accommodation and power to exercise authority, the characters of such start to deform and become corrupted. It was the British politician and historian Lord Acton who wrote in 1887,

"Power tends to corrupt, and absolute power corrupts

---

[18] Shabbath folio:31a, *The Babylonian Talmud*

[19] Isocrates. 3.61 *Isocrates* with an English Translation in three volumes, by George Norlin

absolutely. [20]

The urge to control others becomes a major temptation, one that is often succumbed to. It is sad when we see adherents of other religious traditions forsake the Golden Rule, but it becomes especially tragic when it comes to the Christian religion.

Inflicting religious oppression is foreign to the principles of Christianity. Even when met with the prospect of intense and unrelenting persecution. There is no room for retaliation or vindictiveness. When faced with the prospect of torture and martyrdom for sharing their faith, the Apostles of Christ chose death instead of armed defiance.

Indeed, when Peter rose with a sword and cut off the ear of Malchus to defend his Lord in the Garden of Gethsemane, Christ rebuked him, saying,

> *"Put up again thy sword into his place: for all they that take the sword shall perish with the sword."* [21]

---

[20] Acton, John E. E. D. as quoted in Smith, Peter. *Essays on Freedom and Power*, pg. 7

[21] Matthew 26:52, *King James Version*

With enough preparation it would have been very easy for that small fledgling group of Disciples to create an escape path for their Master and call for reinforcements from sympathizers.

Dozens, if not hundreds of individuals have been healed by the Great Teacher from Galilee, and thousands have been fed miraculously as they listened to His simple yet moving sermons. Judea was always ripe for an uprising, given the great disillusionment of the Jewish establishment with the Roman authorities. This Jesus Christ could have been their ticket to finally buck Rome off their back and secure their complete sovereignty.

Such a Man with the power He had, with the seemingly divine miracles that awed men and women, this "Messiah" could be their savior from the shackles of Roman Imperialism and the might of Tiberius Caesar. But the Jewish leaders eyed the Galilean with contempt and suspicion; their frustration grew from jealousy and the fact that Jesus did not attempt to challenge Roman civil authority. By declaring,

"Render therefore unto Caesar the things which are Caesar's; and unto God the things that are God's,"[22]

---

[22] Matthew 22:21, *King James Version*

Christ disconcerted the mindset of the Jewish religious authorities, for they sought a religiopolitical solution to their subjugation.

Christ would have none of it. He made it clear that worldly civil authority was to be respected and obeyed so long as it did not conflict with the greater authority of the Creator of the Universe. We will revisit this concept in chapter 10 when we study about the "powers that be". The refusal of Christ's involvement in worldly politics is why, when the early Christian Church grew in its infancy, we saw no efforts on the part of the Early Church leaders or Apostles to agitate the status quo on civil leadership and policy. There is no record, whether in Holy Writ, or among primary and secondary historical sources that include the early Church Fathers, that indicate a pressing priority on the part of Church leaders to vie for political office or to change civil laws to reflect Christian ethical and morals standards.

With the rise of Christianity as the state religion of the Roman Empire, this would change. But there remains no attempt by the pre-Constatine era Church to control or even influence civil power to favor Christian ethics; they were content to merely practice their faith whether in peace or opposition, meeting harsh and often terrible persecution. The persecution during the Diocletian era thousands of Christians were put to death, and many more displaced and hunted down.[23]

This is not to say that the early Christians did nothing to defend themselves from accusations of treason and subversion. In fact, early Christians eloquently defended themselves as loyal citizens of the Empire, as we see Tertullian and Origen attempt in various letters to magistrates and fellow believers.[24] It is true, Christians underwent horrible persecution for centuries, leading up to the Edict of Serdica in 311 AD, issued by Emperor Galerius which granted state tolerance to Christianity [25] and officially ended its state-sponsored persecution.

It would have been fine had Christianity been content with toleration. But its uneasy relationship with the Roman civil state would start to become considerably warmer. The Roman Emperor Constantine I came to power in 306 AD but had to share authority over different divisions of the Empire between himself and other claimants. Constantine defeated his co-Emperor, Maxentius, at the Battle of the Milvian Bridge in 312

---

[23] Holmes, Thomas Scott. *The Origin & Development of the Christian Church in Gaul*, ppg. 37-44.

[24] Jensen, Robin M. *Baptismal Imagery in Early Christianity*, ppg. 62-64.

[25] Gibbon, Edward. *The History of the Decline and Fall of the Roman Empire*. Cosimo, Inc. ppg. 132-133.

AD. In that battle it is said he received a revelation to turn to the Christian God for assistance.[26]

The battle saw the death of Maxentius and was a decisive victory for Constantine and his forces, which he saw as a reward for his trust in the Christian God. In response, Constantine began to favor Christianity, and, along with another co-Emperor, Licinius, issued the Edict of Milan in the year after his victory at Milvian Bridge. This edict was a civil declaration of toleration for Christians within the Empire.

This did not make Christianity, however, the official state religion. That would not take place for another sixty-seven years when in 380 AD, co-Emperors Theodosius I, Gratian and Valentinian II issued the Edict of Thessalonica in response to doctrinal schisms within the Church, namely the controversy between Nicene Trinitarians (named after Nicene Creed which affirmed the Trinity and given at the First Council of Nicaea in 325 AD) and Arian Non-Trinitarians (named after Arius, a church leader who taught that Jesus was begotten at some point in time and therefore not eternal).[27]

It was this edict that gave the Christian Church at that time

---

[26] Rohmann, Dirk. *Christianity and the History of Violence in the Roman Empire: A Sourcebook*, pg. 67.

[27] De Laet, Sigfried J., Hermann, Joachim. Ed. *History of Humanity: From the seventh century B.C. to the seventh century A.D.*, ppg. 236-237.

the title "Catholic" (or "universal") Christians. It also established the basis of Church and State union with serious implications for Religious Liberty down the line. Now theological disputes could be handled and settled before civil courts and magistrates with civil punishments dolled out to "heretics" who happened to disagree with the established orthodoxy.

This was the classic HPRS at work. Christians had now shifted from being the persecuted to becoming the persecutors. Ignoring the fact that such an edict would have some serious legal ramifications, the Emperors continued with its issuance with the prodding of Church leaders. No doubt they intended to defend the orthodox faith, however, it would later become a source of grief and anguish for the many who would dare express an opinion that deviated from the established doctrines.

Now with the support of the arm of the state, the Catholic Church would spend the next millennium or so suppressing dissenting opinions and attempting to eradicate perceived heretical sects. To be fair, not all Catholics agree with this notion of defending the faith. This is not an indictment upon members of the Catholic faith down through the ages to today. This is to raise awareness about the origins of this religiopolitical mindset, and why it is inimical the principles of freedom of conscience.

In the words of one great Catholic believer who happened to become elected as the 35th President of the United States of America, spoken to the Greater Houston Ministerial Association before his election:

"I am wholly opposed to the state being used by any religious group, Catholic or Protestant, to compel, prohibit, or persecute the free exercise of any other religion."[28]

John F. Kennedy was merely echoing the First Amendment to our Constitution. Only by enduring the often-tragic lessons of history did America raise the banner of freedom of conscience for all, so that *all*, regardless of religious and non-religious convictions could live peaceably with one another. This is the true American, and as we will discover later, the true Christian spirit.

The pitfalls of propping up Church doctrine with the arm of the state became acutely apparent in the centuries after the passing of the Edict of Thessalonica in 380 AD. The armies of the Empire were mobilized to defend orthodoxy, and the first major victims were the Arians. Many of the Gothic kingdoms

---

[28] Kennedy, John F. *"Speech to the Greater Houston Ministerial Association."* Greater Houston Ministerial Association, 12 Sept. 1960, Houston, TX.

that contended with the Roman Empires adopted Arianism, and the Catholic Church looked to the Imperial war machine to eliminate the heretical kingdoms and establish orthodox hegemony in Europe and its surrounding lands.[29]

The Ostrogoths and Vandals were prominent Arian Gothic Kingdoms that flourished in the 4th-5th century AD. Justinian the Great, a 6th century Emperor of the Eastern Roman Empire rose to defend Christian orthodoxy and began to reclaim the lost territories of the Western Roman Empire. Through the military genius of his commanders such as Belisarius and Narses, Justinian destroyed the once-thriving Gothic Kingdoms, and once again, the orthodox faith had full control over the Empire.[30]

The idea of temporal warfare as a meritorious religious act wasn't fully developed before the 11th century, however.[31] By that time the religiopolitical landscape of the civilized world had changed. Islam rose to become a major power in the Middle East, and quickly conquered the Holy Land from the Byzantines. It was then that Crusades were called to reclaim

---

[29] De Laet & Hermann, pg. 257.

[30] McNeill, William H. *History of Western Civilization: A Handbook*, pg. 209.

[31] Peters, Edward. Ed. *The First Crusade: "The Chronicle of Fulcher of Chartres"*, pg. 8.

the territory to make conditions more favorable for Christian pilgrimage.

This is where the idea of exchanging serving in the Crusader army for merits towards salvation took off. Whereas in previous campaigns and wars, Christian soldiers would have no explicit reward for their risk of life and limb, now the Pope himself offered absolution to the man who would pick up shield, spear, and sword to fight the infidel.[32]

Thousands flocked to join the Crusader cause, and the Holy Wars saw the exchange of possession of the Holy Land several times. In the end, the Holy Land fell into the hand of the Muslims, although the *Reconquista* saw the complete expulsion of Islam from Spain. The Christian Spanish rulers then issued edicts to forcibly convert the remaining Muslims in the Iberian Peninsula to Christianity.[33]

It may be pointed out that Islam also tends to convert by the sword and through other means of coercion. This is true. However, Islam is not beholden to the words of Jesus Christ, whom we Christians consider to be the divine Son of God. Therefore, we hold Christianity to a higher standard than Islam

---

[32] Bongars, Gesta Dei per Francos, 1, 382 f., trans. in: Oliver J. Thatcher and Edgar Holmes McNeal (eds.), *A Source Book for Medieval History*, ppg. 513–517.

[33] Faiella, Graham. *Spain: A Primary Source Cultural Guide*, ppg. 62-64.

as we expect Christians to adhere to the words and principles of the King of Kings. If Christianity seeks a worldly theocracy in the same vein of Islam, it can claim to be no better. We will see why this is in chapter 7 when we discuss the "New Covenant and the Theocracy of the Heart".

The implications of defending orthodoxy with civil means were seen in the various Crusades and Inquisitions meant to stomp out heresy. Thanks to the continuing pervasiveness of HPRS in the general psyche of theologians and politicians of the day, it was easily forgotten that Christianity itself was at one point a hated sect, persecuted and hunted to be silenced and destroyed. But did persecution cause Christianity to perish? To the contrary, it thrived and grew. If the instigators of the Crusades and Inquisitions had retained the historical lessons learned from the past, they would know their efforts in quenching the fires of heresy would be futile with the methods they used.

Now that Christianity had gained political power, she sought to consolidate that power in the hands of a few that would maintain control in the name of defending orthodoxy. Arianism was almost virtually eliminated with the fall of the early Goth Kingdoms, but other perceived heretical movements began to arise that caused consternation to Rome. In response to the lavish lifestyle of those officials that represented the Roman Catholic Church such as priests and bishops, a movement formed in the 12th century AD in southern France called Catharism.

The Cathars, as they were called, had very peculiar beliefs that contradicted many orthodox teachings. At first, Pope Innocent III was content to have missionaries and priests preach strongly against the heresies of Catharism. But these efforts were all frustrated, and Innocent fumed at the murder of his representative Pierre de Castelnau, [34] who was sent to suppress the heresy. In response to the death, Innocent called for a Crusade against the Cathar heretics, also known as the Albigensians, as many of their number hailed from the city of Albi, France.

In mid-1209 AD, warriors seeking Crusader indulgences flocked to the Papal banner, ready to slay heretics in the name of the Pope. A bloody twenty-year campaign to wipe out the Cathars then proceeded with fury, and hundreds of thousands were killed. On July 22, 1209 around 20,000 were killed in the town of Beziers in a massacre of horrific proportions. The Papal Representative that accompanied the Crusader army, Arnaud Amalric wrote,

---

[34] Taylor, Claire. *Heresy in Medieval France: Dualism in Aquitaine and the Agenais, 1000-1249*, pg. 187.

"Our men spared no one, irrespective of rank, sex or age, and put to the sword almost 20,000 people. After this great slaughter the whole city was despoiled and burnt... "[35]

Amalric is also reported to have said in response to the concern that there might be faithful Catholics among the heretics, "*Caedite eos. Novit enim Dominus qui sunt eius*" or "Kill them all...let God sort them out".[36] The slaughter was unimaginable. 20,000 men, women, and even children perished in one day. Comparatively, there were 7,800 killed in 3 days at Gettysburg during the American Civil War,[37] and 2,300 killed per day during the 10 month-long battle of Verdun in World War I.[38] Even if we placed all of the 6 million Jewish victims killed during the Holocaust during the Nazi implementation of the "Final Solution" of 1941-1945, that would mean

---

[35] Sibly, W.A.; Sibly, M.D. *The Chronicle of William of Puylaurens: The Albigensian Crusade and Its Aftermath*, ppg. 127–128.

[36] Headsman (22 July 2009). *"1209: Massacre of Béziers, "kill them all, let God sort them out""*.

<http://www.executedtoday.com/2009/07/22/1209-albigensian-crusade-cathars-beziers/> Retrieved 12 June 2019.

[37] Busey, John W., & Martin, David G. *Regimental Strengths and Losses at Gettysburg*, ppg. 126 & 260.

[38] Heer, H.; Naumann, K. *War of Extermination: The German Military in World War II, 1941–44*, pg. 26.

approximately 4,100 Jews were killed every day.

This is not to downplay the horrific loss of life in the Holocaust, or to demean the sacrifice of soldiers on the battlefields of glory. On the contrary, we see that any loss of life is significant and tragic, and when instigated in the name of Christ it is especially saddening because Christ gave His life so that men, all who are sinners, could be saved for eternity.

Well, one may argue, we do not seek the blood of individuals in attempting to preserve and uphold orthodoxy. We only want proper morality instilled through the influence of the Church upon the State. But religious oppression is exactly what the uniting of Church and State leads to, however innocuous the intentions. Therefore, the American Founders sought hard to uphold the absolute separation of Church and State, as we will see in Chapter 5, "The American Separation of Church and State".

The Albigensian Crusade lasted a whole twenty years, from 1209 to 1229. The total number of victims was estimated to be 1 million.[39] Catharism was wiped out as a belief system, and theological dissidents throughout Europe feared the dreaded Papacy and the armies it could send upon them at the calling of the Pope. Raphael Lemkin, the lawyer who sparked

---

[39] Robertson, John M. *A Short History of Christianity*, pg. 254.

the Genocide Convention and coined the term "genocide" referred to the Albigensian Crusade as, *"one of the most conclusive cases of Genocide in religious history."*[40]

A stain on the character of historical Christianity, the Crusades to root out heresy were only the beginning. The Papal Inquisition initiated by Pope Gregory IX and carried on for several centuries gave the Church a powerful civil weapon against heresy. A church trial was conducted to ascertain the charges of heresy against the accused, and if found guilty, the alleged heretic was allowed to recant and if he or she did, was supposed to be released unmolested with the obligation to conduct penance.

If the heretic was found guilty and did not recant or repent, then the heretic was given over to the secular arm of the state for capital punishment, which included the infamous burning at the stake. This Church and State collusion resulted in many abuses by both church and secular authorities to eliminate opposition at whim. Notorious examples include the elimination of the Order of the Knights Templar and the trial and execution of Joan of Arc.

The Templars were a Catholic military order and served

[40] Lemkin, Raphael. Jacobs, Steven Leonard, ed. *Lemkin on Genocide*, pg. 71.

in the several Crusades in the Holy Land, fighting the Muslim Saracens. Joan of Arc was a French military leader who led France to many victories against the English during the Hundred Years' War. Both the Templars and Joan of Arc were captured and brought before their political adversaries who used the Inquisition to condemn them. Most of the Knights Templar were burnt at the stake by 1312, and Joan of Arc was burnt in 1431 at the age of 19.[41]

Later Papal investigations found them innocent of charges or in the case of the Templars, restored into the sanctity and unity of the Catholic Church; Joan of Arc was declared a martyr and given sainthood. The irony is the very mechanism the Papacy instituted for the defense of the faith caused many innocent believers their lives. This could have all been avoided had the Church harkened to the principles of its foremost Founder, Jesus Christ, who never taught to defend belief in Him with the sword.

Various dissidents of the Roman Catholic Church before the formal emergence of the Reformation met harsh persecutory measures and often torture and death. John

---

[41] Lea, Henry Charles. *A History of the Inquisition of the Middle Ages, Volume 3*, ppg. 337, 301-308.

Wycliffe (circa 1320-1384),[42] an English priest and scholar protested against the corruption and moral abuses of the Catholic clergy. He also translated the Bible into the English vernacular, earning the ire of Rome. Wycliffe's teachings threatened the authority of the Roman Church, and persecution of Wycliffe and his followers began in earnest. Wycliffe himself escaped the Inquisition and died a natural death, but his remains were exhumed and burnt to ashes by representatives of the Catholic Church, and his works also burnt.[43]

The followers of Wycliffe, also known as the Lollards, were not as fortunate. They suffered civil punitive measures and were driven underground. In 1401 the parliament of King Henry IV of England enacted a law entitled, "*De heretico comburendo*" or "Regarding the burning of heretics", aimed at the growing threat of Lollard heresy. It proclaimed in no uncertain terms, theological heretics as subversive to the civil state and condemned any such convicted individuals to death by burning at the stake.

William Sawtey who was a former Roman Catholic priest

---

[42] Wilson, John Laird. *John Wycliffe, Patriot and Reformer: "The Morning Star of the Reformation"*, pg. 18.

[43] *Ibid.*, pg. 230.

who accepted and taught Lollard beliefs was burnt at the stake in 1401 and is considered as one of the first Lollard martyrs. John Badby, a layman who shared Lollard teachings was burnt in a barrel in 1410. [44] The Lollards, heavily persecuted, operated underground for over a century until the Protestant Reformation began, when they were able to assimilate into the growing Protestant movement.

Jan Hus (circa 1369-1415), a Bohemian priest that was influenced by the works of Wycliffe, was the leading figure in the Bohemian Reformation which was a movement that caused political rifts in the Bohemian and Moravian regions of that day. Hus become very influential, and like Wycliffe, took advantage of his position to disseminate his views, critiquing the abuses of the clergy. These views become prominent among the commoners and a few conscientious noblemen.

As the movement grew, the Papacy felt threatened and sought to quell the Hussite sentiments growing in Bohemia. Civil authorities began to execute Hussite believers in 1412, and on July 6, 1415, Jan Hus himself was burnt at the stake, sparking the Hussite Wars that saw Bohemia and Moravia go up in arms. The Hussites were able to resist Catholic domination for a little over two hundred years until the Holy

---

[44] Foxe, John. *Foxe's Book of Martyrs*. London, Day. 1563. Ppg. 312-313

Roman Empire crushed the Protestant army at the Battle of White Mountain in 1620. After the Imperial victory, the Protestant rulership was de-established, and forced conversion to Catholicism took place.[45]

In the next chapter we will analyze the Protestant contributions to Religious Liberty, but we must make it clear not all Protestant movements steered clear of the temptation to conflate the realms of Church and State. Even after major Protestant thinkers had begun to realize the futility of using the state to advance spiritual interests, the involvement of Christianity in civil politics was too great. Protestants who themselves suffered from a heavy dose of HPRS began to persecute Catholics and many of their fellow Protestants, especially during the rise of the Church of England, a state-sponsored Church with the Head of State as its leader.[46]

The Protestants of this day had not yet fully developed the idea of complete religious toleration, but a small faction within Protestantism began to see its civil benefits and Scriptural merit. This idea then continued to grow in earnest, thanks to the reaction over the trail of blood left by the Inquisition, the

---

[45] Walkowitz, Daniel; Knauer, Lisa Mayer, ed. *Memory and the Impact of Political Transformation in Public Space*, Pg. 49.

[46] Coffey, John. *Persecution and Toleration in Protestant England 1558-1689*, pg. 27.

use of religion to further colonialism, and affected peoples' own desire to follow the dictates of their consciences. Soon, the flame of religious freedom lit by Protestantism would grow into a raging fire by the time of the Enlightenment.

CHAPTER THREE

Protestantism and the Enlightenment

THE DIVISION OF THE WESTERN CHURCH into
Protestant and Catholic factions was a direct result of Martin
Luther's protest on the selling of indulgences for the benefit for
the construction of St. Peter's Basilica. Other Reformers
followed suit, such as John Calvin and Huldrych Zwingli,
protesting the perceived injustices of the Roman Catholic
Church and the Papacy.[47]

---

[47] d'Aubigné, Jean Henri Merle. *History of the Reformation in the Sixteenth Century*, ppg. 80-273.

Challenging the authority of the Pope over spiritual matters, Luther appealed to the authority of the Scriptures over man issued mandates and tradition. By doing this, Luther initiated the road towards individual liberty of conscience. The Protestant thinking was that the common man should be allowed to read and understand the Scriptures for themselves, and not need the dictates of popes and priests.[48]

Martin Luther proposed the idea of there being "two kingdoms", God's Kingdom presiding over spiritual matters, and the secular authority, presiding over temporal things. He argues thus,

"God has ordained the two governments: the spiritual, which by the Holy Spirit under Christ makes Christians and pious people; and the secular, which restrains the unchristian and wicked so that they are obliged to keep the peace outwardly... The laws of worldly government extend no farther than to life and property and what is external upon earth. For over the soul God can and will let no one rule but himself. Therefore, where temporal power presumes to prescribe laws for the soul, it encroaches upon God's government and only misleads and destroys souls.

[48] Greider, John C. *The English Bible Translations and History*, pg. 278.

We desire to make this so clear that every one shall grasp it, and that the princes and bishops may see what fools they are when they seek to coerce the people with their laws and commandments into believing one thing or another.[49]

Here it is seen that Luther had a clearer grasp of the freedom of conscience than any major Church thinker before him. He should know; the very political power the Roman Catholic Church wielded during his time allowed for and even encouraged the abuses he protested against. While his philosophy on the matter was still far from granting full freedom of conscience for those of all religious convictions, Luther's idea of separating the two spheres of authority denotes a complete break from Catholic practice on the matter and established the separation of Church and State as a Protestant principle, which, as we will see later, would influence the thinkers of the Enlightenment.

Other Reformers began to pick up on the idea, although to varying extents. John Calvin, for example, had no problem settling a theological controversy using the arm of civil power. On the matter of Michael Servetus, Calvin allowed the use of

---

[49] Luther, Martin. *On Secular Authority: To What Extent it Should be Obeyed.* (1523) No. 3 and 4.

civil force to solve the issue of Servetus' heresy. Servetus maintained a heretical position on the doctrine of the Trinity and was sought by the French Inquisition to face execution.

The Protestant Calvin also condemned the teachings of Servetus, and when the latter showed up in Geneva, where Calvin and his fellow Reformers resided, Servetus was arrested and brought to trial. On October 27, 1553, Michael Servetus was burnt at the stake by the Protestant Republic of Geneva. A former protégé of Calvin, one Sebastian Castellio (1515-1563), was so disturbed by this incident that he published a pamphlet entitled *De haereticis*, under the pseudonym Martin Bellius.

Castellio had seen the effects of the Inquisition in person, witnessing "heretics" being burnt at the stake. A convert to Protestantism from Catholicism, Castellio was one of the first to advocate for the full freedom of conscience in the context of Church and State relations. In his pamphlet *De haereticis* which was addressed to Duke Christoph of Württemberg and published in 1554, Castellio highlights the major issues in using state power and capital punishment to solve theological disputes.

Rebuking the Roman Catholic Church and the Reformers that claimed to protest against her injustices but meted out their similar brand of injustice, Castellio eloquently explains the problem of Church and State collusion in acting as the consciences of men.

> *"Pride is followed by cruelty and persecution so that now scarcely anyone is able to endure another who differs at all from him. Although opinions are almost as numerous as men, nevertheless there is hardly any sect which does not condemn all others and desire to reign alone. Hence arise banishments, chains, imprisonments, stakes, and gallows and this miserable rage to visit daily penalties upon those who differ from the mighty about matters hitherto unknown, for so many centuries disputed, and not yet cleared up."[50]*

Castellio clearly sees the issue as one of theological hubris, unfortunately involving capital punishment. To Castellio, this attitude should be alien to Christianity, and also to the State, which should have no say in matters of spirituality. He saw Calvin's rule over the Protestant haven of Geneva, Switzerland as a theocracy, tragically proven by the very burning at the stake of Michael Servetus. In his pamphlet, Castellio quotes at length Martin Luther's treatise on "The Scope of the

---

[50] Castellio, Sebastian. *On Heretics.* (1554) Translated by Roland Bainton, pg. 3.

Magistrate's Authority", the second part of the pamphlet *On Civil Government.*

Castellio furthermore quotes Johann Brenz (1499-1570), a prominent theologian and Reformer in the Duchy of Württemberg. Brenz explains,

"...unbelief and heresy, so long as nothing else is involved, are subject only to the punishment of the Word of God. If they break loose and commit sedition, murder, or some other crime, then, and then only, are they subject to the correction of the civil sword."[51]

Sadly, because of this Castellio was maligned and ostracized, essentially banished from Geneva and lived the rest of his life in obscurity and poverty in Basel, Switzerland thanks to the political maneuvering of Calvin. Because the voices of the likes of Castellio were muted, and that Luther's and Brenz's works on the matter were largely ignored, the Magisterial Reformers continued to persecute other Protestants, such as the Anabaptist believers who comprised the Radical Reformation.

The Anabaptists believed that believers should be baptized only when they had the ability to confess the faith and make a

---

[51] *Ibid.,* pg. 21.

conscious decision to be baptized. This practice contrasted with the doctrine of infant baptism the majority of other Christians, including Catholics and the Magisterial Protestants adhered to and put them at odds with the mainstream Christian world. They were then subjected to heavy persecution and civil penalties.

To complete the break from Catholicism, Protestantism would need to shed the notion of uniting Church and State entirely, something they would not learn for at least a couple of centuries. It was only through painful trials and tragic lessons that Protestantism would finally complete its separation from the Roman Catholic Church on this matter. But thanks to the works of liberty greats such as Luther, Castellio, and Brenz, we see a wealth of ideas that even the intellects of the Enlightenment referred to many times.

Enter the Enlightenment. Also known as the "Age of Reason", the Enlightening provided an intellectual and philosophical alternative to despotism, monarchism, and church dominance in political affairs. The Enlightenment was born out of a philosophical awakening to the liberty of individual thought in matters of religion, science, and sociopolitical affairs.[52]

Both the Renaissance and the Protestant Reformation were precursors to the Enlightenment; the Scientific Revolution became the catalysts of the Enlightenment, with the astronomical discoveries of men like Nicolaus Copernicus, Galileo Galilei and Johannes Kepler. But what precipitated growing angst among learned men wasn't the discoveries themselves, but rather the Church's reaction to them.

The Catholic Church had a rather difficult time in maintaining its hegemony on Western civilization thanks to the rise of the Renaissance and the Protestant Reformation, creating kinks in the armor of the Catholic religiopolitical machinery. The collaboration of secular and spiritual powers began to weaken, and the Enlightenment hastened its demise.

Men like Thomas Hobbes (1588-1679) and John Locke (1632-1704) promoted theories of human government that advocated for governments based upon the consent of the governed rather than on "divine right". Hobbes differed from Locke, however, in that Hobbes' view espoused a government with a strong central power, consented upon by the governed to protect their rights. Locke envisioned a government with a

---

[52] Sweetman, John E. *The Enlightenment and the Age of Revolution, 1700-1850*, pg. 5.

proper division of powers, and any government that governs without the consent of the people can and should be overthrown.[53]

While the Reformation promoted individual liberty and rights to the spiritual aspect of the conscience, the Enlightenment appealed to the liberty of secular and temporal thought. Both these concepts are essential to the development of the idea of separation of Church and State. The Protestant Reformation sought spiritual freedom, the individual's duty towards his or her conscience was their own business, a covenant between them and their God/gods/themselves. The Enlightenment allowed them to freely express and exercise these views with relative freedom and without fear of being oppressed or prosecuted by a temporal authority.

Luther and Castellio were spiritual greats that helped Enlightenment philosophers like John Locke develop meaningful arguments against the primacy of Church-State authoritarianism and establish a liberal theory of governing based upon the liberty of the individual. This principle is decidedly *Protestant*, and has been since the inception of the name, which was derived from their stance after the Diet of

---

[53] Locke, John. *Two Treatises of Government, On Civil Government,* ppg. 311-312.

Speyer in 1529, when they protested an Imperial ban on the Lutheran faith, demanding that they be allowed to follow their conscience with regards to faith.[54]

In his Letter Concerning Toleration, published in 1689, John Locke eloquently laid out the case for Religious Toleration and Liberty by evoking the Protestant mantra of separating the spheres of Church and State. During his day, Locke saw an increasingly paranoid State sponsored Church, the Church of England, turn a suspicious eye on its giant rival, Catholicism. Both the Anglican and Catholic systems were identical in their overt involvement in secular politics, using statecraft to accomplish their spiritual agendas.

Often, they used their state mechanisms against each other and their dissidents. Thomas Hobbes argued that a state church could help curb social disorder; Locke on the other hand, argued that there should be a diverse marketplace of ideas when it came to religious conviction. Locke's philosophy became the bedrock of some of the clearest theories on Religious Liberty in the modern world, and one that the American Founders relied upon in their quest to establish a free and just society.

---

[54] Taylor, Matthew. *England's Bloody Tribunal, Or, Popish Cruelty Displayed*, pg. 381.

As Locke himself put it,

"I esteem it above all things necessary to distinguish exactly the business of civil government from that of religion and to settle the just bounds that lie between the one and the other."[55]

This distinction was important to the liberties of men; no one man had the jurisdiction upon the conscience of another. Locke's Libertarianism of the human conscience helped propel the Protestant cause down the line, initiating movements that would later demand a separation between Church and State.

For the philosopher with a Christian worldview it had its risks. Deism and atheism arose as strong minority factions within the Enlightenment and grew as time went by. But for all its risks, the "Two Kingdoms" philosophy of separation of Church and State is by far the most Christian view of religiopolitical theory. The practicing of the Golden Rule by Christians towards others of different faiths would be put to the test, and it would bear fruit in the form of a fledgling American Republic, granting religious tolerance as a crucial part of its

---

[55] Locke, John as quoted in *The Oxford Handbook of Secularism,* Zuckerman, Phil & Shook, John, (eds.) pg. 130.

existential identity.

Thanks to the Protestant Movement and the Enlightenment, those that live in America and in the many other nations that developed a similar attitude of religious toleration towards their subjects now enjoy the freedom to worship or not worship according to the dictates of their consciences. The development of the American separation of Church and State was not the mere handiwork of Deists or the Protestants, it was a collaborative effort between Deists and Protestants. This is a freedom that many, down through the ages, could only dream about, and countless numbers of them had been tortured and killed for their faith.

The victims of religious oppression are countless, and they come from all backgrounds and faith traditions. But unfortunately, so are the perpetrators. Muslims, Buddhists, Atheists, Hindus, Jews, Christians, and many, many others. It seems that no one sect, religious believer or not, has been exempted from giving and receiving persecution. The degrees may vary, according to the political influence of any given group, but the point remains this, if we allow the mingling of religious establishments with secular power, we see very adverse results in society.

Yes, we may see an outward conformity of belief and some semblance of civil order as envisioned by Hobbes' work

Leviathan, which argued for a strong, undivided central government, complemented by a state church. But Locke's thesis resounds more with the simple Gospel of the Christian faith. The principles of Christ's Kingdom cannot be enforced by civil political machinery. This is not to say none of the Biblical morals can be rightfully and dutifully enforced as a civil law.

After all, murder, stealing, lying, and marital infidelity are frowned upon in almost any lawful society. And it would be civilly just and right to curb these abuses that infringe upon the rights of others. But as the "two kingdoms" principle suggests, cases that fall outside the purview of civil order, and that which affects no one other than the perpetrating individual who self-consents to the action, and all others that can be classified as "actions of the mind", these cannot be enforced by the worldly magistrate. A more in-depth discussion on the difference between morality and civility is found in chapter 10.

The Enlightenment formed as a reaction to the religious establishment's claim over the consciences of men. Once an interest in art, science, and literature was awakened in the Renaissance, the Protestant era fostered a growing sense in the common man that he had the ability to think for himself and make a conscious effort to understand God's Word not through the lenses of centuries of embellished tradition, but by their reading.

The doctrine of Justification by Faith, a prominent doctrinal fixture of the Reformation was attractive to freedom lovers everywhere. No longer were men confined to believing what God had to say to them via prelates and priests, or by Church traditions. They could read and understand it for themselves. The separation of Church and State makes this possible.

The Enlightenment furthered this concept by providing the philosophical mechanism for which religious and intellectual toleration could be applied to secular states. It is no coincidence that a more vigorous emphasis on the sciences arose, along with more alternative viewpoints such as deism and atheism. Perhaps some would argue that the Inquisition was still preferable than the atheistic communist regimes that brutally suppressed Christianity and other religious beliefs, or the Islamic theocracies that oppress women and promote barbaric behavior towards infidels.

But one thing is clear. It is not the way of Christ to fight tyranny with tyranny.

CHAPTER FOUR

The American Experiment

THE LAND WE NOW KNOW AS the United States of America wasn't always a haven of liberty. We know the historical narrative of Pilgrims and Puritans migrating to the New World to escape the tyranny of the Church of England. While the Pilgrims that landed at Plymouth in 1620 exercised a good measure of religious liberty, as we saw in chapter 1, the Puritans that populated the Massachusetts Bay Colony in 1628 were intolerant of others with different religious views. Charles I granted a Royal Charter for the Massachusetts colonial expedition, which he later came to regret, seeing that the

Puritans became so successful in New England. The king sought to annul the charter in 1635, but, fearing a rebellion, Charles left it untouched, and the Puritans were masters of their new domain.[56]

Quickly forgetting their plight, thanks to HPRS, under the persecutions initiated by Charles' Anglican Archbishop William Laud who persecuted them in England, once given their power the Puritans were themselves determined to conduct their campaign of religious suppression. It is one of American History's most flagrant ironies and one which historians, like myself, are unable to explain. Because the Puritans of Massachusetts executed the Quakers Marmaduke Stephenson, William Robinson, William Leddra, and Mary Dyer for their religious beliefs in the 1660s, New England lost its autonomy when Charles II forbade further executions for religious reasons, revoked the Charter issued by his predecessor. Charles' successor, James II sent a Royal Governor in 1686 to enforce English Law in the Colonies. Three years later, in 1689, the English Parliament passed an Act of Toleration, granting more (although not complete)

---

[56] Wepman, Dennis. *Immigration*, ppg. 9-11.

liberties to individuals of diverse faiths.[57]

So, in an irony of all ironies, England became the champion of more, albeit not complete, religious toleration towards the end of the 17th century, whereas the inhabitants of the Colonies which fled to New England on the pretense of escaping persecution were chastised for their growing intolerance. It wouldn't be until another hundred years later that America would achieve full national autonomy, and the founders of this nation finally understood the light of religious liberty through the legacy of Roger Williams and other trailblazers in the pursuit of freedom.

Roger Williams (1603–1683) is credited as having founded the first Baptist church in America. He is also the founder of the Colony of Rhode Island and the Providence Plantations, one of the original of the Thirteen Colonies to comprise the early American nation. Under the leadership of Williams, the colony flourished as a haven for religious freedom and toleration.[58]

This experiment was formulated from lessons learned while he was still residing in the Massachusetts Bay Colony.

57 Howell, Thomas Bayly & Howell, Thomas Jones, (eds.) *Cobbett's Complete Collection of State Trials and Proceedings for High Treason and Other Crimes and Misdemeanors,* pg. 135.

58 Gaustad, Edwin S. *Roger Williams,* pg. 59.

As a Puritan minister he began to preach what he saw as corruption within the Anglican Church. He served in the Plymouth Bay Colony before returning to Massachusetts where the secular authorities were displeased with his ideas.

It was here that Williams realized the dangers of Church and State collusion. The Massachusetts General Court declared him guilty of sedition and heresy for teaching "dangerous" ideas. He was banished from Massachusetts and in 1636, he made his way towards a tract of land which he purchased in what is now known as Rumford, Rhode Island.

In the years that followed, Williams was able to secure a Charter for the Rhode Island and Providence Colony, despite opposition from Massachusetts officials. It was then that Williams, alongside his friend colleague John Clarke (1609–1676), a fellow Baptist minister, along with and other religious dissenters and exiles like the Quaker Anne Hutchison developed the colony into an experiment in toleration.

It is no surprise that Rhode Island fared well, and the Colony did not descend into the civil chaos predicted by critics of religious toleration in the other colonies. The early civil authorities of the Colony were consistently clear in their desire to separate civil matters from the spiritual, and that no civil magistrate could infringe upon the conscience of any citizen.

Clarke himself, an educated physician and theologian,

wrote the Rhode Island Royal Charter of 1663 which declared,

"that no person within the said colony, at any time hereafter shall be any wise molested, punished, disquieted, or called in question, for any differences in opinion in matters of religion, and do not actually disturb the civil peace of our said colony; but that all and every person and persons may, from time to time, and at all times hereafter, freely and fully have and enjoy his and their own judgments and consciences, in matters of religious concernments, throughout the tract of land hereafter mentioned, they behaving themselves peaceable and quietly...[59]

This brilliant Charter would lay the foundations of the First Amendment of the United States Constitution, and influence men like John Locke to call for greater religious toleration during the Age of Enlightenment. The Rhode Island and Providence Colony became one of the real first experiments in religious toleration in history. Following in the steps of Williams' and Clarke's Rhode Island and Providence Colony

[59] Clarke, John as quoted in James, Sydney. *John Clarke and His Legacies: Religion and Law in Colonial Rhode Island 1638-1750*, ppg. 82-83.

was William Penn's Pennsylvania.

William Penn was the son of English Admiral William Penn, a naval officer who helped restore the English monarchy after the English Civil War. The younger Penn became exposed to Quakerism in England, and, after seeing the minority Quakers being persecuted by established Anglicans and Puritans, became disillusioned with his former Anglican faith and converted to Quakerism, much to his father's dismay.[60]

The elder Penn then chose to disown his son, the younger Penn choosing to eschew his material inheritance and become practically homeless. Although disowned and without a permanent place to stay, the younger Penn still tended to his father's estates in Ireland in the late 1660s, fellowshipping with fellow Quakers. He later reconciled with his father who told him, "Let nothing in this world tempt you to wrong your conscience". In the 1670s Penn networked in Germany and found a willing following of Quaker converts who would later follow him to Pennsylvania.

Like Roger Williams, Penn was an eloquent theologian and thinker. And, like Williams, he was critical of the establishment on religious grounds which did not sit well with

---

[60] Endy Jr., Marvin B. *William Penn and Early Quakerism*, ppg. 93-100.

the English authorities. He wrote several pamphlets decrying the moral and spiritual corruption of the Catholic Church and other magisterial Protestant groups, and especially the Church of England, which succeeded in having him imprisoned in the Tower of London.

The elder Penn, before his death, managed to secure an agreement from the Crown as a favor for his role in restoring the English monarchy. He wrote to the Duke of York, who would later become James II of England, heir to the throne at that time, asking that Royal protection be granted to his son. James' brother King Charles II saw an opportunity to repay the Royal debt the monarchy owed to the Penns.

Charles signed a charter extending a huge land grant to the junior William Penn on March 4th, 1681. The King named the tract of land "Pennsylvania" in honor of the service of the elder William Penn and gave the younger Penn almost complete sovereignty in governing the land. Immediately Penn went to work gathering settlers, and he made Pennsylvania a haven for the religiously persecuted, in similar vein to the Rhode Island and Providence Colony.

Quakers, Baptists, Anabaptists (including the Amish and Mennonites), Lutherans, Catholics, and Jews began to settle into Pennsylvania, coming from nations in Europe embroiled in religious conflict for decades. They thrived in Pennsylvania which guaranteed them the right to exercise their consciences freely. Heavily influenced in his views on Religious Toleration by Enlightenment thinker John Locke, Penn went even further and set the foundation of a progressive civil society, setting up the use of amendments to constitutions to effect societal and civil change without the need for bloody revolutions.

Thanks to men like Rogers Williams, John Clarke and William Penn, the light of Religious Liberty began to shine brighter in the colonies, paving the way for a free Republic in which the conscience of each person would be his own, without the interference of civil authorities. The Protestant Reformation and the Enlightenment would set the way and influence the fledgling New World Colonies in proclaiming religious freedom for all.

By the time the American Colonies were clamoring for national sovereignty and independence, the principle of Religious Toleration was firmly rooted in the would-be United States. Although elements of the old Puritan theocratic mentality still pervaded in many civil circles (as it does today), it was clear that the experiments on Religious Liberty within several of the colonies were a social success. Colonial society did not collapse and fall into anarchy as some critics predicted. In fact, the opposite was true. The progressive policies on freedom of religion paved the way for greater societal peace and harmony in the Colonies. The historical era in which wars were fought over religion had finally ended.

Historians Gary Amos and Richard Gardiner write,

"The Protestant Reformation in Europe and in the American colonies forced people to reexamine the traditional merger between church and government. America in particular was to become the test case for resolving the tension between religious freedom and social conformity."[61]

The American Experiment was a success, and it opened the door for similar policies in nations all over the world. However much a trailblazer America is in the area of freedom of conscience, there is still a danger to fall back into a theocratic backlash against modern societal trends that are disagreeable to the majority. It is very tempting to stunt the progress of liberty to enforce a majority view.

This cannot be so. The Framers of our Constitution made

---

[61] Amos, Gary; Gardiner, Richard, as quoted in "The First Experiments in Freedom of Belief and Religious Tolerance in America", *The Founding*, 28 September 2017.

<**https://thefounding.net/religious-freedom-first-experiments-freedom-belief-america/**> Accessed 2 August 2019.

it plain that there would be no religious test for public office in Article VI, clause 3. The text states,

"...no religious test shall ever be required as a qualification to any office or public trust under the United States."[62]

In today's volatile political atmosphere there is still much controversy over this clause. As of the writing of this volume, several states have constitutions that still contradict this clause and cause some consternation. The States have argued the Article does not apply to them, only to the Federal government. But this no doubt contradicts the intent of the Framers, for why require no religious test for the Federal government and not for the States? Examples include:

Arkansas State Constitution, Article 19, Section 1 states:

"No person who denies the being of a God shall hold any office in the civil departments of this State, nor be competent to testify as a witness in any Court."

---

[62] US Constitution, Article IV, Clause 3. *Legal Information Institute.*

<**https://www.law.cornell.edu/constitution/articlevi**> Accessed 15 August 2019.

The State of Maryland Declaration of Rights, Articles 37 & 39 state:

"That no religious test ought ever to be required as a qualification for any office of profit or trust in this State, other than a declaration of belief in the existence of God; nor shall the Legislature prescribe any other oath of office than the oath prescribed by this Constitution."

"That the manner of administering an oath or affirmation to any person, ought to be such as those of the religious persuasion, profession, or denomination, of which he is a member, generally esteem the most effectual confirmation by the attestation of the Divine Being."

Mississippi's State Constitution contains a General Provision in Article 14, Section 265 that:

"Denial of [a] Supreme Being [is a] disqualification to hold office."

North Carolina's State Constitution contains the following, from Article VI, Section 8:

"The following persons shall be disqualified for office: ...any person who shall deny the being of Almighty God."

The Pennsylvania State Constitution contains a provision for Religious Freedom in Article I, Section 3 granting that "All men have a natural and indefeasible right to worship Almighty God according to the dictates of their own consciences", but then confiscates the same rights from atheists and agnostics seeking public office in Section 4:

"No person who acknowledges the being of a God and a future state of rewards and punishments shall, on account of his religious sentiments, be disqualified to hold any office or place of trust or profit under this Commonwealth."

South Carolina's Constitution in Article XVII Section 4 states,

"No person who denies the existence of a Supreme Being shall hold any office under this Constitution."

Likewise, the Tennessee State Constitution puts it this way

in Article IX Section 2,

> *"No person who denies the being of God, or a future state of rewards and punishments, shall hold any office in the civil department of this state."*

Finally, the Texas State Constitution mostly echoes the 3rd clause of Article VI of the United States Constitution, but contains an addendum not found in the national document. Article I, Section 4 of the Texas Constitution states,

> *"No religious test shall ever be required as a qualification to any office, or public trust, in this State; nor shall any one be excluded from holding office on account of his religious sentiments, provided he acknowledge the existence of a Supreme Being."*

The Constitutions of Mississippi, South Carolina, and Texas are ambiguous, as one can argue for atheists, the ultimate "supreme being" is oneself. However, all these examples are equally disturbing because they represent an attempt to add at least one more qualification to the 3rd clause of Article VI of the national constitution that simply is not there.

Religious freedom must be for all, and if one belief system is threatened, all are threatened. In the following chapter, we will explore how this was the intent of the Framers of the American nation, and why it is important to maintain their legacy through today and onward.

CHAPTER FIVE

The American Separation of

Church and State

IT IS INTERESTING THAT THERE IS STILL significant debate over the topic of Church and State separation in American society. That issue should have been settled a long time ago. It is understandable, however, that shifting societal trends make application of this principle very contentious. There is an ongoing war between elements on one end, those on the Right who wish to return to what is essentially Puritan era morals and civil enforcement of such, and on the Left, a growing libertine sentiment looking to normalize their views of morality and impose them upon society.

Both extremes are deplorable, and thankfully they represent, at least at this point in history, a minority. According to a recent US poll, 6% identify with the Far-Right, and 8% identify with the Far-Left.[63] However, the shifting tides of the political pendulum, major world, and local incidents may trigger a series of events leading to an unbalance of power in the nation and the world. This is the reason for the need to safeguard the guarantees of the American Constitution. There is also a very Scriptural need for this practicality, which we shall explore later in the chapters where we will discuss applying Biblical principles to our modern Church and State relations.

The American separation of Church and State grew out of a reaction to the perceived injustices of the Church's collusion with the State to stifle dissent. In the last chapter, we

---

[63] Fleishman, Glen. "The Far Right Represents Only 6% of U.S. Citizens, Study Says. 67% Make up the 'Exhausted Majority.'" Fortune Magazine 22 October 2018.

<https://fortune.com/2018/10/22/far-right-americans-just-six-person-study-says/> Accessed 22 August 2019.

discussed the examples of Roger Williams, John Clarke, and William Penn, influential men who developed the first real civil experiment in religious freedom and toleration. Their ideas were driven by the bitter yet eye-opening trials of persecution. While Enlightenment philosopher John Locke set the ideological grounds for the principle, Williams, Clarke, and Penn applied these principles in civil practice.

Williams was exiled, Clarke was imprisoned and fined, both experiencing trials because of their opposition to Puritan doctrines. They later helped establish the first Baptist Churches in America. Penn, as a Quaker, was imprisoned several times and it was only his father's heavy influence on the Crown and the providence of the Almighty that he was able to lead and transform Pennsylvania into a haven of religious freedom and toleration.

Through these harsh experiences, these men were determined not to follow their colonial predecessors in developing HPRS. They knew full well that the Pilgrims and Puritans were themselves fugitives fleeing the persecution of the Anglican establishment. Once left to manage their administration, the Puritans proved to be just as tyrannical as their Anglican persecutors. The circle of violence would then never end.

Williams, Clarke, and Penn, along with countless others

with dissident religious views and were persecuted for their faith became determined to strike at the heart of the matter, the union of Church and State. Williams was the first to use the analogy of a wall separating the two. So it was, in all ironies that a devout Christian and founder of the Baptist Church in America, not an atheist, who so strongly called for a wall to be erected between Church and State.

For Williams, the role of the Earthly government was to deal solely with civil matters. The compact he wrote as an agreement with other settlers in Providence contained no mention of God. This was not to indicate a lack of piety on the part of Williams and company. On the contrary, it indicated a desire for an even higher ideal, one where God, and not man, would be the Arbiter of His Kingdom, the Kingdom "not of this world". Man had proven himself too incapable to govern other men over the things of God, so the highest Authority would be God Himself, working on the individual conscience.

In his dispute against the Reverend John Cotton, who had him exiled from Massachusetts on pain of death, Roger Williams penned the work entitled, "The Bloudy Tenet of Persecution", arguing against the evils and dangers of Church and State union. Williams wrote,

"Mr. Cotton ... hath not duly considered these following

particulars. First, the faithful labors of many witnesses of Jesus Christ, existing in the world, abundantly proving, that the Church of the Jews under the Old Testament in the type and the Church of the Christians under the New Testament in the anti-type, were both SEPARATE from the world; and that when they have opened a gap in the HEDGE, or WALL OF SEPARATION, between the garden of the Church and the wilderness of the world, God hath ever broken down the WALL itself, removed the candlestick, and made his garden a wilderness, as at this day. And that therefore if He will ever please to restore His garden and paradise again, it must of necessity be WALLED in peculiarly unto Himself from the world, and that all that shall be saved out of the world are to be transplanted out of the wilderness of the world and added unto His Church or garden... a SEPARATION of Holy from unHoly, penitent from impenitent, Godly from unGodly."[64]

Here Williams makes a clear distinction between the system designed for worldly government and that of Christ's Church, and argues that there is an ideological and spiritual

---

64 Williams, Roger. *The Complete Writings of Roger Williams*, ppg. 227-228.

wall of separation between the world and the Body of Christ. This wall, if tampered with, in Williams' view, will be demolished by God and allow the growth of corruption within the Church and State alliance. The only way for Christianity to be pure, then, is to erect this wall of separation and keep the Church separate from the world, or the State.

To further understand the concept of Church and State Separation, we must first analyze the Amendment to our Constitution that contains the clauses which establish this principle. Some argue that the term "separation of church and state" cannot be found in the Constitution. This is true, that passage is not in the Constitution verbatim. But the principle certainly is, and it is this principle that Thomas Jefferson referred to in his letter to the Danbury Baptist Association in 1802 when he wrote,

"Believing with you that religion is a matter which lies solely between man and his God; that he owes account to none other for his faith or his worship; that the legislative powers of government reach actions only and not opinions, I contemplate with sovereign reverence that act of the whole American people which declared that their legislature should make no law respecting an establishment of religion or prohibiting the free exercise

thereof,' thus building a wall of separation between Church and State.[65]

This wall was not to be "one-directional", meaning that the flow of influence could travel only one way as with a controlled valve. The wall was meant for the complete and total separation of the two spheres of governance, in accordance with Protestant and Enlightenment principles. This principle is practical; if Church was to influence political policy, and we use the word "Church" here to denote an established religion, then the natural consequence would be that this Church will be able to drive public policy with impunity at the detriment of other religious belief systems that do not share the same conscientious convictions.

There is a sentiment that the "wall of separation" should allow Church influence in civil government but stop civil government involvement in Church matters. While this may seem like an acceptable compromise for Evangelical Christians that seek to wield some civil power to fulfill the Gospel Commission, it doesn't provide a solution to a real problem. Ecclesiastical favoritism is that problem and it was supposed

---

[65] Jefferson, Thomas. *"Letter to the Danbury Baptists."* Received by Nehemiah Dodge, Ephraim Robbins, & Stephen S. Nelson, 1 Jan. 1802.

to have been sufficiently addressed by the Establishment Clause of the First Amendment to our Constitution, which is discussed in a moment. It is best to note,

"'Separatists' like the Quakers, Baptists, Methodists, and Mennonites were opposed to establishment of religion on principle, but even those who were believers in a close alliance between church and state (Presbyterian, Congregationalist, Lutheran, Catholic) began to see the values of separation in societies where they were not the dominant church. Thus, the religious heterogeneity of the American colonies helped to undermine the religious establishments..."[66]

Remember that the reason why the Baptists, the Quakers, and other Christian-based faiths, not to mention all the non-Christian ones were persecuted was because the state was influenced by the Puritans. If we are to believe that the Church should be able to influence the government and not the other way around, we set up a standard that is not realistically possible. How so? It is because the nature of government is to

---

[66] Butts, Robert Freeman. The Education of the West: A Formative Chapter in the History of Civilization, pg. 304.

regulate civil mores and standards. Therefore, the best scenario is for the civil government to be religiously neutral and not partial to any one religious' system, Christianity or otherwise.

The concept of a "one-way" wall is exemplified in articles by organizations seeking to render ineffective the notion of church and state separation. For example,

"...the religion provisions were added to the Constitution to protect religion and religious institutions from corrupting interference by the federal government and not to protect the civil state from the influence of, or overreaching by, religion."[67]

To illustrate this strange concept, with which many Judeo-Christians are somehow enamored, think of a magical wall that allows people from one side through, but not from the other. This is not a wall at all, if it can even be called close to one, but more properly like a net, catching the fish of civil

---

[67] Dreisbach, Daniel. The Mythical "Wall of Separation": How a Misused Metaphor Changed Church–State Law, Policy, and Discourse. *The Heritage Foundation* 23 June 2006.

<**https://www.heritage.org/political-process/report/the-mythical-wall-separation-how-misused-metaphor-changed-church-state-law**>
Accessed 20 August 2019.

government influence to keep them from affecting the Church. But the water of Church influence on government passes through freely. This idea is neither supported by the Constitution nor is it in any way Biblical. Both the American form of government *and* the New Testament concept of Christ's Kingdom *not of this world* demand a complete separation of church and state.

Conservative theory of the "wall of separation" according to *The Heritage Foundation:*

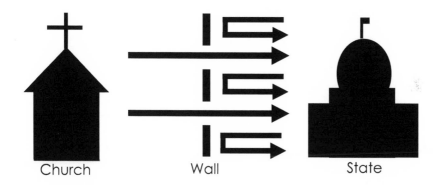

Church   Wall   State

The Constitutional "wall of separation" and the Framers' intent and true Protestant and Enlightenment version:

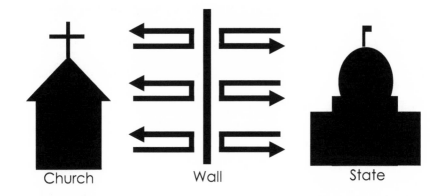

Church   Wall   State

It is because of the historical lessons detailed in previous chapters that the Constitution was formulated as such when it comes to the issue of religion. To better understand what the Constitution is telling us, it behooves us to quote verbatim the exact passage of contention:

"Congress shall make no law respecting an establishment of religion, or prohibiting the free exercise thereof..."

Of course, the amendment continues to offer other guarantees, but the section that concerns the topic of this book is given above. Clearly outlining the boundaries from which the state should operate, it is here that we derive the concept of "separation of church and state". Leading up to the drafting of the Bill of Rights, there was some debate over the nature of religion, among other inherent rights, in the fledgling American government.

The First Amendment protected five basic liberties; the freedom of religion, freedom of speech, freedom of the press, freedom of assembly and the freedom to petition the Federal government to redress grievances. The first of those liberties, that of the freedom of religion, was emphasized by James Madison. On June 8, 1789, Madison completed his first draft of a Constitutional Amendment to guarantee religious freedom in which he wrote:

"That in article 1st, section 9, between clauses 3 and 4, be inserted these clauses, to wit, the civil rights of none shall be abridged on account of religious belief or worship, nor shall any national religion be established, nor shall the full and equal rights of conscience be in any manner, or on any pretext infringed."[68]

This draft had to go through the gauntlet of Congressional approval, and upon receiving it, Congress went to work to modify it to its satisfaction. Back and forth it went, and on August 15th of that year, Samuel Livermore of New

---

[68] Madison, James. *Congressional Register*, 8 June 1798, Vol. 1, pg. 427.

Hampshire suggested going with,

"Congress shall make no laws touching religion, or infringing the rights of conscience".[69]

On August 20th, the representative from Massachusetts, Fisher Ames suggested that it read,

"Congress shall make no law establishing religion, or to prevent the free exercise thereof, or to infringe the rights of conscience".[70]

This was closest to the current wording, but it still had to hurdle the Senate which from which arose several proposed changes, mostly regarding excluding "one religious sect" and "denomination", all of which were voted down. Ames' language survived and was ratified by the states as part of the First Amendment on December 15, 1791.[71]

---

[69] Sikorski, Robert (ed.) *Prayer in Public Schools and the Constitution, 1961-1992: Government-Sponsored Religious Activities in Public Schools and the Constitution*, pg. 68.

[70] Davis, Derek H. *Religion and the Continental Congress, 1774-1789: Contributions to Original Intent*, pg. 19.

[71] *Ibid.*, pg. 82.

It was a long time coming. With many painful lessons learned along the way. Lessons that are in danger of being forgotten, thanks to a healthy dose of agenda-driven HPRS. It has been suggested that the Founders of America intended it to be a Christian nation. A myriad of quotations is then offered from the Founders that seemed to tout this notion. But we must be very careful here. Context, intent, and motivation are key. We must also remember we cannot take one man's opinion, no matter how important he is to the foundation of the nation as the law. The text of the Constitution and the Bill of Rights that formed its first 10 amendments were heavily debated by Congress and the Senate.

To gain a purer understanding of the intent of the American Fathers, we are to piece together our view from the consensus of the day that put the Constitution in place. Context is very important here, and with the astute politicians of the American Founding era remembering all the lessons that went into the civil experiments which established religious liberty, it is not very difficult to ascertain why the Framers avoided using religious language when dealing with the Constitution.

First, the Constitution was designed to govern a civil and not theocratic society. Second, if the Framers intended to allow religion to freely influence the civil government, there would be endless debates on the nature of this influence, and which religious sect would have political power over the other.

We do acknowledge, however, the presence of God in the Declaration of Independence. There, the invoked Creator is acknowledged as the Author, not of social mores but individual liberty and independence. This has fascinating and profound implications. The foremost implication is that God is the Author and Designer of free will and individual conscience as invoked in the Declaration of Independence, while man, doing his best to render a stable and civil society is the author of Earthly laws as invoked by the Constitution.

The dichotomy is striking. The Framers declared independence by appealing to a Higher Authority, while framing laws under the Constitution and governing their fellow man by appealing to the secular democratic process with appropriate checks and balances. This separation of Church and State is deliberate and designed to avoid the excesses of ecclesiastical entanglement in state affairs by religiopolitical powers like the Roman Catholic Church and the ostensibly Protestant Church of England.

Only this interpretation passes muster in the face of the primary sources surrounding the founding of this great nation. It also provides a remarkable balance on the question of faith and politics. It is a direct rebuke of state-sponsored religion and state-sponsored atheism. The former by the Constitution's

90

demand to keep the state from creating laws that favor an establishment of religion, and the latter by prohibiting any laws that keep the citizen from exercising their right to free conscience and the freedom to worship as one pleases.

The idea that man is free to his conscience is transcendent; the idea that man needs to be governed by his fellow man on social matters is a secular affair, and thus the Divine is not referenced in the Constitution.

"The Constitution fashioned in 1787 is a secular document. There is no mention of God, Jesus Christ, or a supreme being anywhere in the document. A minority faction of delegates pressed for some type of recognition of Christianity in the Constitution, but their views were rejected."[72]

To determine the Framers' original intent and their real attitude to church and state separation, let's look at the primary sources from the pioneers and founders of America. Indeed, some of these quotations are very disturbing to the Christian Nationalists, but they inform the very basis for the foundations

---

[72] Boston, Robert. *Why the Religious Right is Wrong about Separation of Church & State*, pg. 62.

of our Liberty. Please note, that these quotations are from men that come from the Age of Reason, and while they supported the tenet of separation of church and state they remained believers in Christianity, or the very least Deism, which acknowledges a Creator. Here are the aforementioned quotes:

"When a religion is good, I conceive it will support itself; and when it does not support itself, and God does not take care to support it so that its professors are obliged to call for help of the civil power, 'tis a sign, I apprehend, of its being a bad one."[73]

"We have abundant reason to rejoice that in this Land the light of truth and reason has triumphed over the power of bigotry and superstition, and that every person may here worship God according to the dictates of his own heart. In this enlightened Age and in this Land of equal liberty it is our boast, that a man's religious tenets will not forfeit the protection of the Laws, nor deprive him of the right of

---

[73] Franklin, Benjamin (1817). *"The private correspondence of Benjamin Franklin, LL.D, F.R.S., Minister Plenipontentiary from the United States of America at the court of France, and for the Treaty of Peace and Independence with Great Britain, comprising a series of letters on miscellaneous, literary, and political subjects written between the years 1753 and 1790, illustrating the memoirs of his public and private life, and developing the secret history of his political transactions and negociations"*, pg. 69.

attaining and holding the highest Offices that are known in the United States."[74]

"Where the preamble declares, that coercion is a departure from the plan of the holy author of our religion, an amendment was proposed by inserting 'Jesus Christ,' so that it would read 'A departure from the plan of Jesus Christ, the holy author of our religion;' the insertion was rejected by the great majority, in proof that they meant to comprehend, within the mantle of its protection, the Jew and the Gentile, the Christian and Mohammedan, the Hindoo and Infidel of every denomination."[75]

"The legitimate powers of government extend to such acts only as are injurious to others. But it does me no injury for my neighbor to say there are twenty gods, or no god. It neither picks my pocket nor breaks my leg."[76]

---

[74] Washington, George; Sparks, Jared (ed.) (1838) "The Writings of George Washington: Being His Correspondence, Addresses, Messages, and Other Papers, Official and Private", pg. 202.

[75] Jefferson, Thomas. (1821) "Autobiography of Thomas Jefferson". Works, Volume 1, pg. 71.

[76] Jefferson, Thomas. (1781-1785) Notes on the State of Virginia, query 17.

"Who does not see that the same authority which can establish Christianity, in exclusion of all other Religions, may establish with the same ease any particular sect of Christians, in exclusion of all other Sects?"[77]

"Thank God, under our Constitution there was no connection between church and state."[78]

"Every new and successful example, therefore, of a perfect separation between the ecclesiastical and civil matters, is of importance; and I have no doubt that every new example will succeed, as every past one has done, in showing that religion and Government will both exist in greater purity the less they are mixed together..."[79]

"The civil Government, though bereft of everything like an associated hierarchy, possesses the requisite stability, and performs its functions with complete success, whilst the number, the industry, and the morality of the priesthood,

---

[77] Madison, James. *A memorial and remonstrance, on the religious rights of man; written in 1784*, pg. 5.

[78] Polk, James K. *The Diary of James K. Polk During His Presidency*, pg. 353.

[79] Madison, James. *Letter to Edward Livingston from James Madison*, 10 July 1822.

and the devotion of the people, have been manifestly increased by the total separation of the church from the State. [80]

"In politics, as in religion, it is equally absurd to aim at making proselytes by fire and sword. Heresies in either can rarely be cured by persecution." [81]

"We should begin by setting conscience free. When all men of all religions shall enjoy equal liberty, property, and an equal chance for honors and power we may expect that improvements will be made in the human character and the state of society." [82]

Arguments are made by the Christian establishment that a secular philosophy is causing this rift between Church and State, and that it is something that Christian scholars and administrators should resist. However, there is powerful evidence in both our American founding and in the Scriptures

---

[80] Madison, James. *Letter to Robert Walsh*, 2 March 1819.

[81] Hamilton, Alexander. *The Federalist*, No. 1, pg. 2.

[82] Adams, John. *The Works of John Adams Vol. 8: Letters and State Papers 1782 - 1799*, pg.197.

themselves that present a case against mingling the two in the context of a New Testament civil atmosphere.

James Madison himself, the "Father of the US Constitution" said it best in his letter to Edward Livingstone, quoted with larger context:

"Notwithstanding the general progress made within the two last centuries in favour of this branch of liberty, & the full establishment of it, in some parts of our Country, there remains in others a strong bias towards the old error, that without some sort of alliance or coalition between Government & Religion neither can be duly supported. Such indeed is the tendency to such a coalition, and such its corrupting influence on both the parties, that the danger cannot be too carefully guarded agst. And in a Government of opinion, like ours, the only effectual guard must be found in the soundness and stability of the general opinion on the subject. Every new & successful example therefore of a perfect separation between ecclesiastical and civil matters, is of importance. And I have no doubt that every new example, will succeed, as every past one has done, in shewing that religion & Govt will both exist in greater

purity, the less they are mixed together."[83]

Here, Madison isn't trying to diminish the purity and freedom of Christianity (and consequently other religions) by separating it completely from the machinery of the State; to the contrary, he argues rightly so that separation ensures its preservation and integrity.

A young Madison developed this attitude in response to some egregious violations of the liberty of conscience he witnessed in Colonial America. To Madison, the civil influence of the Anglican denomination and its Puritan allies over the American colonies was an extension of British rule and tyranny. He envisioned a civil state where religious dissent and competition would flourish, and therefore, British corruption and dictatorship would consequently dissolve.

In 1774, Madison received word of several Baptist preachers being jailed for preaching and passing out pamphlets of their beliefs, and this set him off on a crusade for Religious Liberty. Enraged, he wrote to his good friend and colleague William Bradford, the future US Attorney General:

"Union of religious sentiments begets a surprising

---

[83] Madison, James. *Letter to Edward Livingstone.*

confidence, and ecclesiastical establishments tend to great ignorance and corruption; all of which facilitate the execution of mischievous projects...That diabolical, hell-conceived principle of persecution rages among some; and to their eternal infamy, the clergy can furnish their quota of imps for such business. This vexes me the worst of anything whatever. There are at this time in the adjacent country not less than five or six well-meaning men in close jail for publishing their religious sentiments, which in the main are very orthodox. I have neither patience to hear, talk, or think of anything relative to this matter; for I have squabbled and scolded, abused and ridiculed, so long about it to little purpose, that I am without common patience. So I must beg you to pity me, and pray for liberty of conscience to all.[84]

If there is any lack of clarity as to Madison's hostility to Church and State union, this should have settled the case. Unfortunately, as with the Puritan origins of American mores, there remains a religious strain, predominantly Christian in character, looking to impose a "Christian" interpretation on American civil law, the very philosophy Madison sought to

---

[84] Madison, James. *Letter to William Bradford, Jr.* 24 January 1774.

combat in his lifetime. This attitude of intentionally opposing a major Framer of our Constitution is very unAmerican.

In the Post-Civil War Reconstruction America, a movement formed to get the United States Constitution reworded to explicitly acknowledge "God" and "Jesus Christ". In 1864, leaders of several Protestant denominations founded the "National Reform Association" or NRA (not related to the "National Rifle Association") in an attempt to amend the Constitution to state,

> *"'We the people' would acknowledge 'Almighty God as the source of all authority and power in civil government, the Lord Jesus Christ as the Ruler among nations, His revealed will as the supreme law of the land, in order to constitute a Christian government...'"*[85]

The crisis of the Civil War and Slavery almost succeeded in eliminating the wall between Church and State, thanks to a growing agitation in the North arguing for Divine support in the abolition of slavery. The movement was tempered by practical considerations, the difficulties

---

[85] Miller, Randall M.; Stout, Harry S.; Wilson, Charles Reagan (1998). *Religion and the American Civil War*, pg. 122.

encountered during Reconstruction, and the realization that the South itself used Christian religious justification for their practice of slavery and their right to secession.

The Wall of Separation has withstood assault after assault by the religious establishment; however, this does not mean it is wholly impervious, thanks to threats of impending amendments or full repeal of the religious freedom clauses. By that time, a crisis beyond that of the Civil War, or the 20th clashes between Democracy, Fascism, and Communism would have to be in place to stir an American population recalcitrant towards the safeguards of the American principle of Freedom of Conscience.

Americans have to be consistently vigilant, opposing with pen, voice and vote attempts to destroy this foundational American pillar that keeps corruption, persecution and tyranny at bay, and allows us to exercise our sacred rights to conscience, whether one is a Christian, Muslim, Hindu, Buddhist, Jew or Atheist. If there is anything that defines America, this is the most basic and distinguishable, with many other nations of the world following our example over the centuries. The "One Nation under God" should be the "One Nation where one can be free to choose their god".

As Joshua, the leader of Israel after Moses, grew feeble and old, he addressed the throng of Israelites at Shechem. At that time, Israel was the very Theocracy of God, under the direct leadership of the King of the Universe, and Joshua was the mere facilitator. But even under the direct leadership of God Joshua gave the Israelites the freedom of choice:

"...choose for yourselves this day whom you will serve, whether the gods which your fathers served that were on the other side of the River, or the gods of the Amorites, in whose land you dwell. But as for me and my house, we will serve the Lord."[86]

If a Theocratic Israel can give men the freedom to choose, why not the United States of America, which is not under the direct leadership of God?

---

[86] Joshua 24:15, *New King James Version*

CHAPTER SIX

The Old Covenant Theocracy

NO CHRISTIAN IN THEIR RIGHT MIND would suggest that the Old Testament Covenant would still be in force today. The very existence of Christianity is hinged on the New Covenant, the basis of which is Christ Himself, the Author and very Foundation of the New Covenant. But why are we discussing this topic in a book about Religious Freedom?

Simple. Bible believers need to understand how the Old Covenant Theocracy relates to the government of Israel past in contrast to the New Covenant understanding that Christ's Theocracy is "not of this world". Christians, especially the politically inclined ones, tend to forget and dilute the lines between the two in a classic example of HPRS.

This results in mass confusion especially in the area of Church and State relations, creating conflicts that could have been solved had one paid close attention to Biblical teaches on the matter. To be fair, most Christians understand we are no longer under the Old Covenant but the New.

The New Testament Book of Hebrews tells us in reference to the Old Covenant:

"He has made the first obsolete. Now what is becoming obsolete and growing old is ready to vanish away."[87]

Further reading of the Book shows why the Old Covenant was obsolete. The author of the Book of Hebrews writes about how the Earthly Sanctuary, or the Tabernacle, was commissioned by God as a type of divinely ordered service to be fulfilled by the Israelites. It shows how the services were conducted, and why.

The service was performed by men ordained in the

---

[87] Hebrews 8:13, *New King James Version*

priesthood, and specific instructions were given regarding the ceremonies and practices conducted by these men. But then it explains that Jesus Christ is the ultimate High Priest, and the rest of the Earthly Sanctuary system is a typification of the anti-type, the true Sanctuary and Tabernacle in Heaven (see Revelation 15:5).

The same goes without saying regarding the civil governance of men. Under the Old Covenant, ancient Israel, as mentioned before, was a Theocracy under the direct governance of God Himself. Yes, He appointed Judges to govern over His People, but these Judges had a direct line to God, making them not the rulers, but rather the repositories of governance whom God entrusted to carry out His will in every single case.

Moses was the first Judge of Israel along this line. Under the direct guidance of God, Moses led the Children of Israel out of the bondage of slavery in Egypt and took them to the wilderness for refuge and they sought shelter under the shadow of the famed Mount Sinai where Moses received the Ten Commandments as is well known among all with any contact with the major Abrahamic Faiths.

In Exodus 24 we see exactly where the Old Covenant was cemented and ratified by the People of Israel:

"So Moses came and told the people all the words of the Lord and all the judgments. And all the people answered with one voice and said, 'All the words which the Lord has said we will do.'" - verse 3.

Strong's Concordance for the word "covenant" in this context is the Hebrew "בְּרִית" or bĕriyth (H1285), which means: "covenant, alliance, pledge", or, in common language, one can use the word "agreement". In essence, the Children of Israel made a pledge or agreement to do everything the Lord told them to do in the "Book of the Covenant" in which Moses wrote the words of the Lord. In verse 7–8 it says,

"Then he took the Book of the Covenant and read in the hearing of the people. And they said, 'All that the Lord has said we will do and be obedient.' And Moses took the blood, sprinkled it on the people, and said, "This is the blood of the covenant which the Lord has made with you according to all these words."

Israel placed itself under the direct governance of God and promised it will abide by the covenant between it and God. Moses sealed the agreement with the blood of sacrificial animals, and hence was the Old Covenant formed. The Book of the Covenant contained the ordinances for sacrificial services, the ceremonial system ordained by God for practice by the Israelites, and a penal civil code which, by today's standards, seem considerably harsh.

However, its level of hardhandedness seems pretty reasonable given that Israel was witness to the very acts of God, first in the salvation of the Hebrews from Egyptian slavery, next in the miracles that God wrought on behalf of Israel on their journey into the Promise Land. It would be folly for any Israelite to consider violating any of the moral and civil codes imposed upon them in the *prima face* evidence of God's benevolence towards them in their past and present.

As Jesus Himself would explain later on,

"For everyone to whom much is given, from him much will be required."[88]

The very fact that Israel was a direct witness to the power and might of God gave them much more the responsibility for their strict adherence and obedience to His every Word. Much was given to ancient Israel, so, therefore, much would be required of them.

---

[88] Luke 12:48, *New King James Version*

This was the Old Covenant concerning civil measures. God Himself was to be ruler over His Earthly People. His Judges were to be His entrusted servants the prophets through which He would impart His will. It was not always to be so. The Israelites grew tired of the direct Theocracy method and decided to switch to a more indirect Theocratic Monarchy government as evidenced in 1 Samuel chapter 8.

Here is where the Old Testament Israelites got into a bit of trouble. God Jehovah declares to His servant, Samuel the Prophet,

"Heed the voice of the people in all that they say to you; for they have not rejected you, but they have rejected Me, that I should not reign over them."[89]

Here God is essentially telling Samuel He was going to allow Israel to have their way, but before that, Samuel was to pronounce to the people the consequences of choosing a worldly king to rule over them. Samuel warns them,

"This will be the behavior of the king who will reign over you: He will take your sons and appoint them for his own

---

[89] 1 Samuel 8:7, New King James Version

chariots and to be his horsemen, and some will run before his chariots. He will appoint captains over his thousands and captains over his fifties, will set some to plow his ground and reap his harvest, and some to make his weapons of war and equipment for his chariots. He will take your daughters to be perfumers, cooks, and bakers. And he will take the best of your fields, your vineyards, and your olive groves, and give them to his servants. He will take a tenth of your grain and your vintage, and give it to his officers and servants. And he will take your male servants, your female servants, your finest young men, and your donkeys, and put them to his work. He will take a tenth of your sheep. And you will be his servants. And you will cry out in that day because of your king whom you have chosen for yourselves, and the Lord will not hear you in that day." – verses 11-18.

It was a dire warning, with grave overtones but the people would have their way (verse 19). As to what logic the Israelites had in mind when rejecting the direct voice of God who led them to victory after victory and placed them in the very land they enjoyed and prospered in goes beyond reasoning.

Whatever their reasoning was, God told Samuel to go

ahead and give in to the people's demands. This was, of course, because God in His benevolence still gives His people freedom of choice even in the face of blatant disobedience to His precepts, commandments, and will. Most students of the Bible should know what happens next. Saul, the son of Kish from the tribe of Benjamin was chosen. Those who know the story of the first worldly monarch of Israel will know his story ends in tragedy, rocked with multiple scandals, an obsessive jealously of his son-in-law David, and disobedience to God.

But Saul was, at the time of his coronation, honorable and godly, with God Himself telling Samuel that the Benjamite would

"...reign over My people."[90]

Again, we see the principle of freedom of choice in the choosing of Saul as King of Israel. God, in His foreknowledge, knew ahead of time that Saul would fall from grace and almost ruin the kingdom. But He wanted His people to learn a valuable lesson, that earthly kings, no matter how devout and obedient can still fall and leave a realm in tatters.

In the choosing of an earthly king over the Heavenly

---

90 1 Samuel 9:17, *New King James Version*

King, the Old Testament theocracy of Israel would fall apart. When Moses presented the Book of the Covenant to the people, and they agreed to be wholly obedient to the word therein, they had to hold themselves to the strictest of standards. There are, of course, many parts to the Book of the Covenant, the majority are shadows of things to come, such as the ceremonial laws that specified the way in which the ceremonies of sacrifice and atonement were carried out.

But another aspect of the covenant was the Moral Law, known as the Decalogue for its ten laws specifying a guideline and definition of what sin is. So the Moral Law outlines the boundaries of righteous living and sin (see Romans 7:7), while the Ceremonial Law outlined the basic steps and regulations surrounding the remission of sins through the Sanctuary service and pointed to the future sacrifice of Jesus Christ on the cross.

When we are talking about the Old Testament Covenant concerning today's social and political atmosphere there is very little correlation. That is why there is a need to apply New Covenant principles in today's society. There is no more True earthly theocracy led by God Jehovah anymore. This is where many conservative Christians, Jews, and Muslims tend to err. They think that God is in some way directly reigning over worldly political kingdoms when in fact no earthly repository can claim the direct guidance of God in a political sense.

The Kingdom of Jesus Christ is most certainly *NOT OF THIS WORLD*. This is why Jesus Christ is going to come back to this earth to bring His *Kingdom from Heaven* to replace the inadequate and fallible kingdoms of this world. When conservative Christians, Jews, and Muslims clamor for worldly influence and political power, they are in essence repeating the mistake of ancient Israel in demanding a worldly king to reign over them.

This is how the Old Covenant failed. The very agreement that Israel went into before Moses and God was constantly being violated. Their disobedience increased and increased, and once they had a worldly leader appointed, things went downhill whenever these worldly leaders did not harken to the voices of God's prophets and messengers. Even when godly kings came into power, they could not completely stem the tide of growing rebellion and disobedience of the people towards God. There were not enough godly kings to keep Israel and Judah from falling, and eventually they would fall into exile to Assyria and Babylon respectively. Samuel prophesied what was to come, and Israel did not listen. Will the faithful Christian believers of the United States of America and other nations around the world make the same mistake?

Will we make God the ruler of our lives by giving our

worship directly to Him without any worldly proxies, whether pope, prelate, or worldly king or president? By entrusting the righteousness of the nation to human leaders instead of personal and individual obedience through our consciences to God, we are making the same mistake, and woe to post-21st century Christians who suffer from HPRS. By whittling away at the wall separating Church and State, many Christians are unknowingly creating a greater problem than what they believe they are solving. They are returning to an Old Covenant view of theocracy which has been done away with by Christ who assured His beloved ones,

> *"Let not your heart be troubled; you believe in God, believe also in Me. In My Father's house are many mansions; if it were not so, I would have told you. I go to prepare a place for you. And if I go and prepare a place for you, I will come again and receive you to Myself; that where I am, there you may be also. And where I go you know, and the way you know."*[91]

Christ has made it clear that His Kingdom is not one

---

[91] John 14:1-4, *New King James Version*

built by human hands. While the Christian pilgrims flocked by the thousands in medieval times to visit temporal sites and relics, the Bible tells us we are pilgrims on this *earth*, making our pilgrimage towards a heavenly land. The Book of Hebrews tells us,

> *"But now they desire a better, that is, a heavenly country. Therefore God is not ashamed to be called their God, for He has prepared a city for them."*[92]

The Kingdom of God is not the United States of America. Or the United Kingdom. Or Russia, Spain, France, or even the Vatican. The Kingdom of God is not of this world. The American Framers knew the consequences of establishing a state Church. They fought to keep Old Covenant Theocracy ideology at bay. They knew, including James Madison, that religion when infused with the political power of the state would create a tyranny that would trample upon the consciences of men and stamp out liberty.

This is why any incursion by the church upon the state must be resisted. In the previous chapter we saw that some argue that the First Amendment was meant to keep government

---

92 Hebrews 11:16, *New King James Version*

out of religion, but not religion out of government. They fear that by conceding to complete separation of church and state they would give way to secular and even atheistic government that would impose its will upon the people. But if the Free Exercise clause is always respected this can never happen. The Establishment and Free Exercise clause are give-and-take; the government can't respect an establishment of religion by laws, and in exchange for this it also cannot by law, restrict free practice of religious beliefs.

Those seeking to unite Church and State are retrograding back into an Old Covenant ideology. And it's an agreement with God they cannot keep, and, if the testimony of the Old Testament is to be believed, ancient Israel could not keep. Humans just make sinful choices, and without the leading of the Holy Spirit, all they do is sin and violate laws, both moral and civil. There needs to be a divine solution to a human problem. If we look to worldly leaders, we only exacerbate the problem. And just as the Old Covenant Israelites could not abide by the covenant they made with God, modern Old Covenant Christians who seek to impose their values by civil law instead of through personal influence and leading of the Holy Spirit of God will suffer the same fate.

The kingdom of Israel, after many, many decades of disobedience to God, following the example of their evil kings (and the inability of the righteous ones to enact righteousness among their subjects as they are only human), fell to the growing Assyrian Empire. Shalmaneser V, king of Assyria laid siege to Samaria and his successor, his brother Sargon II captures it in 722 BCE.[93] A sad and tragic end to one part of the kingdom which was supposed to represent God's kingdom on Earth.

The kingdom of Judah fell much later in 597 BCE after a lengthy seven-year siege of Jerusalem by the Babylonian King Nebuchadnezzar.[94] Tragic ends to the kingdom that would be God's on earth, all because they desired a fallible human leader, so naturally, the graces of the kingdom would continue on an overall spiral downward, even when under the leadership of godly kings like David, Solomon, Jehoash, Hezekiah, and Josiah. If we allow God to rule His subjects directly upon individual hearts, we cannot go wrong. It is time to ditch the Old Covenant philosophy and embrace the Protestant Christian New Covenant teaching on church and state.

---

[93] Becking, Bob. *The Fall of Samaria: An Historical and Archaeological Study*, ppg. 21-26.

[94] Lipschitz, Obed. *The Fall and Rise of Jerusalem: Judah Under Babylonian Rule*, ppg. 52-56.

CHAPTER SEVEN

The New Covenant Theocracy

of The Heart

IN THE FINAL YEARS OF THE KINGDOM of
Judah, God called upon the prophet Jeremiah to prophesy to
the people. God knew the impending destruction of the Judiac
kingdom was near, and He sent a messenger to warn the people
and its leaders of what was to come. Sadly, the people did not
listen to the prophet and the king had him imprisoned for

predicting the upcoming demise of the realm.

This was the straw that broke the camel's back, and complete sovereignty was never again given to the theocratic Judaic kingdom. Judah would go into exile into Babylon, and became subjects to the subsequent world empires, including Medo-Persia, Hellenistic Greece and Imperial Rome. The years of probation for which Israel was granted an earthly king to govern the people of God was over. God determined that a heathen king would be no worse than the kings that governed Israel and Judah.

This is quite an indictment on the ideology of theocratic monarchy the people raved about to Samuel in their attempts to have a king installed. Sadly, Christians over the centuries have not learned from the mistakes of Israel's past. From cries of "*Deus Vult*" ("God wills it!") during the First Crusade to the Holy Land to the "Divine Right of Kings", "God save the King/Queen" and today's "In God We Trust", the concept of God-endorsed civil leadership is seen in every epoch of history since the dawn of Christianity.

Do we know that God is on our side as a nation? Just because we envoke "God" in our nation's constitution or legal pronouncements does it make it so? Even Hitler's Nazi government carried endorsements from every major Christian denomination, the Lutheran and Reformed churches in

Germany at that time endorsed the government, and eventually so did the Catholic Church, thanks to Hitler's lip-service to "Christian" values.[95]

Only a minority resisted Naziism, including the "Confessing Church" who declared their duty was to God and His Word, and not any worldly leader, and certainly not a madman such as Hitler. One of the more well-known members of the Confessing Church was the theologian Dietrich Bonhoeffer, who the Nazis imprisoned for speaking against the regime and who they eventually executed for alleged collaboration in the July 20th plot on Hitler's life in 1944.[96] Christians ought to be careful in politics, never to enter into the presumption that God is pleased by the mere invoking of His name in secular political circles.

God is more pleased, if the Scriptures are to be believed, that we honor His kingdom in Heaven through His authority on earth His church, and not a presumptive secular one that is on this earth. Christian Nationalism runs into the conundrum of which "Christian nation" is truly led by God, several of which find themselves on opposite sides of the battlefield.

---

[95] Lindemann, Albert S.; Levy, Richard S. (eds.) Antisemitism: A History, ppg. 200-204.

[96] Schlingensiepen, Ferdinand. Dietrich Bonhoeffer 1906-1945: Martyr, Thinker, Man of Resistance, ppg. 351-378.

While not the official motto of the United States until July 30th, 1956 after being signed into law by President Dwight D. Eisenhower, the saying "In God We Trust" has been around since the American Civil War[97] and sounds similar to the Prussian motto "*Gott mit uns*" ("God with us"), used by the German Wehrmacht in World War I and World War II.

Catholic German soldiers inevitably killed Catholic American soldiers on the shores of Normandy, and Lutheran American soldiers killed Lutheran German soldiers at the Battle of the Bulge. They all served, worshipped, prayed to, and believed in the same God. For which *kingdom* did each soldier die for? Was it the kingdom of Christ? Nay, it was for the kingdoms of men. They fulfilled their duties in their relative spheres, but we must not conflate our obligation to man with our obligation to God.

The reason purportedly Christian nations war against each other (and against other heathen or atheistic nations) is not out of any sense of Christian duty or fight for identity or even defending the "will of God", but because such states are not "Christian" nations at all, but very earthly kingdoms with very worldly priorities and goals. This is what the

---

[97] McDowell, Stephen K.; Beliles, Mark. *In God We Trust: Tour Guide Featuring America's Landmarks of Liberty*, ppg. 226-227.

conscientious Christian must understand when knowing the difference between the kingdom of God and men.

Now this book is not about dissecting or criticizing Just War theory or advocating for pacifism. In fact, I would argue that there is a place for patriotism and even nationalism in the proper sphere, which will be discussed in a later chapter. The very principles of Christ teach us even Christians have duties to the civil states. But we must be careful in fulfilling our duties and render our dues where we should, because if we are not careful, we may be feeding a Beast that we never intended to.

The New Covenant, aside from its implications of soteriology, that is, the theology of salvation, teaches the ruling of the Holy Spirit in the believer's heart. The New Testament is replete with statements indicating the importance of the Holy Spirit in governing the believer's life. The Apostle Paul, writing in the Book of Romans, chapter 8 verses 1-5 tells us,

"There is therefore now no condemnation to those who are in Christ Jesus, who do not walk according to the flesh, but according to the Spirit. For the law of the Spirit of life in Christ Jesus has made me free from the law of sin and death. For what the law could not do in that it was weak through the flesh, God did by sending His own Son in the likeness of sinful flesh, on account of sin: He condemned

sin in the flesh, that the righteous requirement of the law might be fulfilled in us who do not walk according to the flesh but according to the Spirit. For those who live according to the flesh set their minds on the things of the flesh, but those who live according to the Spirit, the things of the Spirit."

We can understand that the Moral Decalogue is the moral standard of the universe. It shows to us what right and wrong is (Romans 7:7), according to the government of the Heavens, where God Himself reigns and is thus immutable. Stealing is wrong in any universe imaginable, and in a universe where God reigns, certainly worship of false deities is objectively wrong as well. Therefore, the Law of God is not replaceable. It forever delineates what is right and wrong in both the Old and New Covenants.

We discussed why the Old Covenant failed; the Israelites did not abide by their agreement with God. It wasn't the promises or even the Law of God that failed, it was the people that purported to keep His precepts and commandments that failed. They failed their end of the agreement. Therefore, there was the need for a New Agreement, a new covenant.

When the last sovereign stronghold of God's people was besieged by the pagan Babylonians, panic overthrew the people. False prophets preached that God would protect and defend the Judaic kingdom despite their outward disobedience and rebellion. Jeremiah was the lone outlier, the unpopular preacher of doom. But no one wanted to listen to him. They wanted assurances of God's support and defense, because after all, God defended Jerusalem before from the mighty army of the Assyrian King Sennacherib in 701 BCE, the Biblical account testifying to 185,000 Assyrian dead.

> *"And it came to pass on a certain night that the angel of the Lord went out, and killed in the camp of the Assyrians one hundred and eighty-five thousand; and when people arose early in the morning, there were the corpses—all dead. So Sennacherib king of Assyria departed and went away, returned home, and remained at Nineveh."*[98]

So utter was Sennacherib's defeat at Jerusalem that he went back home without having completely overtaken Judah, despite conquering a vast majority of the Judaic cities. God intervened on behalf of Judah because they harkened to the leading of God. But such was the presumption of the Judeans under King Zedekiah if they thought God would do the same

---

[98] 2 Kings 19:35-36, New King James Version

for them even while they refused to repent. Jeremiah endeavored to spare the people from a more horrible fate than that which would befall them, but it was futile.

The Old Covenant was shattered. Israel was absorbed into the Assyrian culture and the ten tribes were considered "lost" to history. The Judeans were allowed more cultural autonomy within the Empires that ruled over them, and the line of David's descendants continued through the centuries until a little babe was born in a lowly manger in Bethlehem. God gave a vision of this to Jeremiah, and a promise of a New Covenant and agreement with Israel. So even while the ashes of the ruins of Jerusalem were yet smoldering, God makes a promise to His people:

"Behold, the days are coming, says the Lord, when I will make a new covenant with the house of Israel and with the house of Judah—not according to the covenant that I made with their fathers in the day that I took them by the hand to lead them out of the land of Egypt, My covenant which they broke, though I was a husband to them, says the Lord. But this is the covenant that I will make with the house of Israel after those days, says the Lord: I will put My law in their minds, and write it on their hearts; and I will be their

God, and they shall be My people.[99]

It broke God's heart to allow His people to endure this exile. But as difficult as it was, it had to happen for God's will to be fulfilled. The Old Covenant was destined to always be inadequate. Salvation could never be bought by the works of man even in the Old Covenant. Neither could the blood of sheep, bulls, and goats wash away the sins of man. All the ceremonies pointed to the coming Messiah who would be the

"…propitiation for our sins, and not for ours only but also for the whole world."[100]

But what does this all have to do with freedom of conscience? We know the Gospel of salvation is the gist of the New Covenant, and it behooves every Christian to understand the free gift of salvation by grace through faith. And this is where the real kicker is when it comes to religious liberty and freedom of conscience. The free gift of salvation cannot be forced on anyone. It has to freely be chosen. Of course, some Calvinists may disagree with this conclusion, and we can agree

---

[99] Jeremiah 31:31-33, *New King James Version*

[100] 1 John 2:2, *New King James Version*

to disagree. The Gospel of Christianity is not something that is to be disseminated by the point of the sword.

There are many egregious examples of Christians forcing non-believers to convert or suffer persecution and hardships, past and present. Even Pope Benedict XVI admitted that "unjustifiable crimes" were committed when Western civilizations colonized the Americas, often under the garb of Christianity.[101]

Of course, many other religious groups are guilty of the same thing, the Islamic conquests come to mind. But then again, Christianity's uniqueness lies in the unequivocal loving nature of the Person of Jesus Christ, who, while able to summon hordes of mighty angels to frighten and subjugate heathens and compel them to worship the true God, died for sinners instead.

It is no surprise then, that the New Covenant revealed to Jeremiah includes the promise that God's Laws will be written on the hearts of His people. The author of the Book of Hebrews echoes this Covenant in the New Testament in reference to the ministry and sacrifice of Christ,

---

[101] Fisher, Ian. "Pope Concedes Unjustifiable Crimes in Converting South Americans". *New York Times,* 24 June 2007.

<https://www.nytimes.com/2007/05/24/world/americas/24pope.html> Accessed 24 July 2019.

"But the Holy Spirit also witnesses to us; for after He had said before, 'This is the covenant that I will make with them after those days, says the Lord: I will put My laws into their hearts, and in their minds I will write them', then He adds, 'Their sins and their lawless deeds I will remember no more.'"[102]

As we can see clearly, God wants the principles of His kingdom kept in the hearts of men. The Laws of God's government should be in our hearts, and not Capitol Hill! In later chapters, we will discuss the role of civil government in society, but when we talk about where God's kingdom is supposed to be today under the New Covenant, it is in our hearts, where the Spirit resides in the believer, and the Spirit is not of this world. Christ's kingdom can refer to His physical kingdom, which is Heaven itself, but also the presence of His character in the hearts of those that receive Him in their lives.

"Now when He was asked by the Pharisees when the kingdom of God would come, He answered them and said, 'The kingdom of God does not come with observation; nor

---

102 Hebrews 10:15-17, *New King James Version*

will they say, 'See here!' or 'See there!' For indeed, the kingdom of God is within you.'"[103]

This presents a complication for those still under the Old Covenant mentality of civil government. External laws can govern external actions. But they can never influence the heart. The Christian religion teaches, or at least should teach, that the solution to moral and societal woes is a change of heart. Jesus Himself said,

"What comes out of a man, that defiles a man. For from within, out of the heart of men, proceed evil thoughts, adulteries, fornications, murders, thefts, covetousness, wickedness, deceit, lewdness, an evil eye, blasphemy, pride, foolishness."[104]

The Christian who follows after Christ sees the wickedness that pervades society today. It manifests not only in spiritual, but also in social wrongs. Is there a place for tangible action? Is there a need for civil laws to constrain criminality? Of course! But what we need to remember is that

---

[103] Luke 17:20-21, *New King James Version*

[104] Mark 7:20-22, *New King James Version*

emphasis needs to be placed on the separation of the two spheres of governance; the sphere that governs God's kingdom of the heart, and the sphere of man's civil governance of society. We will study more about this concept in chapter 10 when we discuss the "powers that be".

Today, under the New Covenant, there is no more divine blessing on an Earthly theocracy. That was part of the Old Covenant which was failed by man. By installing human heads of state to arbiter over both spiritual and civil matters Israel created a system that was doomed for failure. The kingdom was split in two, the kings of both split kingdoms were mostly evil, and even under the most righteous of rulers could not elevate the nations back into the highest favor of God. They then fell into exile, laying in wait for the coming of the Messiah, the King of kings, and Lord of lords who rules a Kingdom not of this world.

Under the New Covenant Theocracy of the Heart, Jesus, the King of the Universe, is to rule supreme in the hearts of His followers. There is no New Testament Biblical mandate to create civil laws to force a democratic society to conform to Christian norms. Those who remain in unbelief are not to be constrained to believe by legal coercion or force. Such methods should be foreign to the Christian believer seeking to share his faith. There is no Scriptural support for a government that

128

unites Church and State under the New Covenant. What the New Covenant's proposed government is, is Christ's reign over individual hearts. There can be no worldly substitute.

CHAPTER EIGHT

The Folly of Worldly

Christian Nationalism

THERE IS A PORTION OF AMERICAN society which suggests that America is a "Christian Nation". To the extent that the primary religious traditions and values of the land are led and informed by Christianity, this is true. However, to describe America as a "Christian Nation" in its laws and mechanisms is venturing into dangerous and unconstitutional ground. There is no Biblical support to create any Christian civil state. And the Establishment Clause explicitly precludes this idea.

But that doesn't stop a subset of Americans from trying. By emphasizing the Free Exercise Clause (in their version "free exercise" only pertains to their exercise of faith and not others'), this subset ignores the other clause and seeks for preferences towards a Judeo-Christian legal framework. This is against both the principles of this country and what is even more concerning to the Christian, is that it is against the principles of Holy Writ. Christians, while retaining the ability to be loyal to their respective countries, must be careful not to give their state the designation of a Christian kingdom.

If the lessons of the medieval Inquisition weren't enough, there are many scriptural reasons to avoid the Christian Nationalism folly. Matthew 21 tells of the story of how Jesus rode through Jerusalem,

"Lowly, and sitting on a donkey" (verse 5).

Greeted by hundreds, maybe even thousands the people proclaimed,

"Hosanna to the Son of David! 'Blessed is He who comes

in the name of the Lord!' Hosanna in the highest!" (verse 9).

Jesus paraded through Jerusalem, not in flashy pomp and a royal retinue, but on a lowly donkey. Yet still, the Spirit moved upon the people to greet their King.

Christ could have paraded all the way to Herod's palace, or the Roman governor's residence, stage a successful coup d'etat and ruled from a worldly throne. But the Kingdom of the Son of God was again, not of this world. Jesus was not interested in a political position. The only throne He seeks to occupy is the throne in our hearts. Jeremiah saw this, even as ancient Jerusalem was falling apart around him, and God gave him the vision of a New Covenant of the New Testament.

This is why Christian Nationalism, in a worldly context is folly. True Christian Nationalism is concerned only about the *nation above*, the citizenship of which is ratified by having our Lord and King occupying our hearts. When American nationalists and patriots refer to their so-called "Christian" heritage, they often forgot or overlook this. It is fine to be loyal to an earthly nation, and imperative to be loyal to the heavenly one, but to conflate the two will become disastrous. It is idolatry to put in place of God your national pride and belief that your national laws are sanctioned by the Creator. We must respect civil laws as loyal citizens, but we must also realize that civil laws can be amended and repealed, but God's Law cannot.

America has thrived as a nation dedicated to separating Church and State and being the haven of the persecuted and oppressed. As such, she has welcomed immigrants of all colors, backgrounds, and religious beliefs. This is her strength in the sphere of civil and social relations. This arrangement is blessed because it is Scriptural, as seen in the preceding chapters. Christ's Kingdom is not of this world, and His government is residing in our hearts through the presence of the Holy Spirit. There is, again, no Scriptural mandate to place Jesus at the head of our legislative halls and court buildings. He shuns all earthly thrones. The only throne He wishes to occupy, is the throne in our hearts.

Worldly Christian Nationalism will result in the uniting of Church and State. It will be a system where Christianity, at least in its purest form, will not be exalted, but where man and his ideas of what "Christianity" is, would be exalted instead. The late evangelist Billy Graham saw the dangers of melding Church and State together in the 1980s, commenting on the rise of the Religious Right to *Parade Magazine* on February 1, 1981:

"I told [Jerry Falwell] to preach the Gospel. That's our

calling. I want to preserve the purity of the Gospel and the freedom of religion in America. I don't want to see religious bigotry in any form. Liberals organized in the '60s, and conservatives certainly have a right to organize in the '80s, but it would disturb me if there was a wedding between the religious fundamentalists and the political right. The hard right has no interest in religion except to manipulate it."

Graham's remarks echo James Madison's sentiments regarding the purity of both government and religion, and they are now a warning for an America that does not know how to separate its politics from its religion and vice versa. To illustrate how the inability to understand simple Scriptural principles and the principles that informed the founding of America can skew one's political views, we offer a litany of primary quotations from influential people in circles that wish to eliminate or circumvent the Establishment Clause of our First Amendment to the Constitution.

R. J. Rushdoony, founder of Christian Reconstructionism and founder of the Chalcedon Foundation wrote,

"The state must become Christian and apply Biblical law

to every area of life, and apply the full measure of God's law..."

"The goal is the developed Kingdom of god, the New Jerusalem, a world order under god's law."[105]

Rushdoony is considered an influence in the Religious Right and has started a movement looking to effect a marriage between the religious and political Right-wing,[106] the very maneuver Graham observed and lamented in the '80s. Rushdoony is somewhat ambiguous about his support for a complete Christian domination of the civil state, for he balances the quoted examples above by defining the "state" as an individual, and not a civil government. Still, he is looking forward to a worldly solution to moral ills, and it is no wonder his successors have become more and more insistent on a Christian overthrow of the worldly state.

No, the worldly state must not become Christian. Individuals, not governments, are called to be followers of Christ. Christian Reconstructionists, while being advocates of

---

[105] Rushdoony, Rousas J. *The Institutes of Biblical Law*, ppg. 323 & 357.

[106] McVicar, Michael J. *Christian Reconstruction: R. J. Rushdoony and American Religious Conservatism*, pg. 195.

small government, are somehow able to reconcile their theory of limited government to their idea that the state must enforce Biblical Law (which would require a strong government). If we were to follow true civil libertarian principles it is the individual that must apply Biblical Law, not the state. The tenuous alliance between political self-governance and the religious Right with their desire to use the state as a vehicle for propping up Christianity will crumble, because Church and State do not mix, any more than the holy and the worldly cannot mix.

Rushdoony's son-in-law and Reconstructionist heir-apparent, the economist Gary Kilgore North offers more explicit ideas in the pursuit of a Christian Kingdom on earth. Writing in *Political Polytheism*, published in 1989 North suggests,

"The long-term goal of Christians in politics should be to gain exclusive control over the franchise. Those who refuse to submit publicly to the eternal sanctions of God by submitting to His Church's public marks of the covenant–baptism and holy communion–must be denied citizenship, just as they were in ancient Israel."[107]

---

107 North, Gary. *Political Polytheism: The Myth of Pluralism*, pg. 87.

Modern readers would be more aghast at his other suggestions, such as:

"That modern Christians never consider the possibility of the reintroduction of stoning for capital crimes indicates how thoroughly humanistic concepts of punishment have influenced the thinking of Christians."[108]

This may all seem very fringe, but Gary North is a fixture in the Libertarian Party and the Tea Party, a political movement dedicated to shrinking the state and ending the Fed. A one-time associate of Congressman Ron Paul of Texas, North is clear with his intentions; the eradication of the secular state and the establishment of a Christian Theocracy based on Old Covenant principles. Working with the Christian homeschool movement, North explains their stratagem:

"So let us be blunt: we must use the doctrine of religious liberty to gain independence for Christian schools until we

---

[108] As quoted by Olsen, Walter. "Reasonable Doubts: Invitation to a Stoning: Getting cozy with theocrats", *Reason*, 1 November 1998.

<**https://reason.com/1998/11/01/invitation-to-a-stoning/**> Accessed 23 June 2019.

train up a generation of people who know that there is no religious neutrality, no neutral law, no neutral education, and no neutral civil government. Then they will get busy in constructing a Bible-based social, political and religious order which finally denies the religious liberties of the enemies of God. "[109]

At least North is honest and blunt. Too blunt. But it does give us an insight as to the Bible-twisting strategies of North and the Christian Reconstructionist movement. Now let us dissect what this man is saying in these quotations. In his view Christians must use "the doctrine of religious liberty" to gain "exclusive control over the franchise" and once that end is met to deny "the religious liberties of the enemies of God", and that stoning is an appropriate Christian method of capital punishment. Is this Christian thinking? Most certainly not, and it is a pernicious doctrine that has no place in New Covenant thought and practice. When men picked up stones to throw at a woman caught in the act of adultery, did Jesus pick a stone Himself and throw it at her? No, He did not, even if He was the most qualified and worthy to do so. Instead, He rebuked those

---

[109] North, Gary. (1982) *Christianity and Civilization: The Failure of American Baptist Culture*, pg. 25.

that gathered and said,

"He that is without sin among you, let him first cast a stone at her."[110]

This is exactly why the civil government cannot be mixed with true Christian concepts, which should be applied to individuals and not States. In the eyes of Christ, we are all sinners, and He came to save us from the consequences of sin and immorality by the imputation of His own perfect, sinless life upon ours. Legally, a forgiven Christian is sinless, His sins paid for by Jesus. A civil government and state can't implement this system. It is not the purview of the civil government to forgive sins. Civil crimes require a legal remedy of civil justice, while sins against God's Higher Law require a different remedy altogether, one which the works of man cannot acquire, nor his sufferings and any Earthly penance.

If Christian Reconstructionists want to stone ingrates, drunkards and adulterers, if they want to initiate a civil legal system based upon Old Covenant Theocratic Laws and legal justice, then they would need to be sinlessly perfect to cast that first stone.

---

[110] John 8:7, *King James Version*

Now, we would be disingenuous to suggest all political conservatives desire this end, and we make no claim even close to this. But as we can see, the road to uniting Church and State and complete theocracy gets slipperier the more it is traveled upon. It starts with a temptation, albeit with good motivations, to bring people to follow Christ by establishing civil laws favorable to Christians and their allies. Then more laws are enacted, supposedly to enforce "Biblical morality". Then the persecution starts. Everyone who is not a Christian gets a funny look, might get told they act or sound funny. Laws begin to hamper the religious rights of others, making it hard for them to practice the dictates of their consciences. But it's okay because at least Christians have their right to free exercise, right?

Then imprisonments and fines. Then execution for the heretics. And it doesn't stop there. Since we've already gone that far down the road, we might as well establish laws that protect Christian "orthodoxy". We begin to see the demolishing of Christian denominations, enforcing a doctrinally sound Christendom through civil statutes and regulations. Perhaps a fine if you conscientiously could not believe in the Trinity or imprisonment if you worked on Sunday. It all sounds far-fetched and out-of-the-ballpark, even for a lot of politically conservative individuals. But once you go down that slippery slope, it can get impossible to stop.

This is not just an indictment on some politically conservative individuals. Some Liberals are also guilty of enforcing a version of their beliefs on those that disagree with them, wishing to diminish the free exercise of Christians (and other conservative religions), and what happens is they end up inflaming the Christian Reconstructionists and those on the Religious Right. Both sides inflame each other, swinging the political pendulum dangerously close to either extreme. Whether it's the conservative that pushes the "Free exercise clause" or the liberal that emphasizes the "Establishment clause", we fall out of balance if we disregard both and free America will be no more. People of all beliefs should be able to freely co-exist and offer respect to one another's views on the social plane.

Of course, this is easier said than done. Different religious beliefs and worldviews have views that are often mutually exclusive of one another. However, all should have the right to speak against another's views and vice-versa. This is the purpose of the "Free exercise clause". So, if people can resist the temptation to go beyond words and start threatening another person's life or health, then all is good. The problem is, this is not always the case. We will look into more solutions in the subsequent chapters, but what we need to understand is that America's identity isn't based on a particular faith, it is based on the principle of Liberty for all, whether one is Christian, Muslim, Jew, Hindu, Buddhist, Wiccan or atheist. Ironically, this should make America the most Christian nation for abiding by the principles of Christ who declared, "my Kingdom is not of this world".

True Americans and Christians recognize the right of all to follow the dictates of their consciences. Yes, Christians have the Gospel Commission, but we are commanded explicitly to make disciples through baptism. Nowhere in the Scriptures is baptism forced or coerced; all instances recorded a willing participant, embracing the New Covenant of faith in Christ. Unfortunately, many prominent American politicians are Christian that do not understand the Christian concept of separating the Church from the State and it results in very muddled political views that are dangerous if put in practice.

Former governor of Alaska and one-time 2008 Vice-Presidential candidate Sarah Palin misunderstood these principles when she quipped on Bill O'Reilly's show "The O'Reilly Factor" in 2010 that we should

"Go back to what our founders and our founding documents meant — they're quite clear — that we would create law based on the God of the bible and the ten

commandments."[111]

This is definitely *not* what the Founders had in mind, even though the majority of them were devout Christians and all had some acknowledgment of a god. They were all cognizant of the dangers of Church and State union, and it was very evident in our First Amendment to the Constitution.

It is not accurate, safe nor right for the Religious Right to claim the Founding Fathers of America sought a "Christianized" legal framework for America. For one thing, the Right has no concept of what Christianity is if they believe it means to enact intolerance for any belief except for the one they accept as true. If conservatives believe Christian culture is on the decline, then they must revive it, not in legislative halls but their individual hearts. The true Christian culture has no room for civil religion.

What many don't realize is that "civil religion" (or religious nationalism) is very much a Pagan, not Christian, concept. Mixing Religion and State is anything but Christian. Professor of Sociology at Yale University Philip S. Gorski points out that,

---

[111] Quoted by Lapore, Jill. *The Whites of Their Eyes: The Tea Party's Revolution and the Battle over American History*, pg. 157.

"While the peoples of Rome enjoyed a great deal of religious freedom, they were nonetheless obligated to take part in the civic rituals of the Empire...The refusal of the early Christians to take part in the Roman cult was one of the principal reasons, perhaps the principal reason, why they were subject to periodic persecutions."[112]

The Pagan Romans sought loyalty to their state by requiring their subjects to conduct religious rituals indicating their continued allegiance to the Empire, and those that did not adhere were persecuted. Gorski continues by dryly pointing out,

"Nor did the Christianization of the Empire bring an end to religious persecution; it simply shifted their target — from the Christians to the 'pagans'".

The HPRS cycle comes full circle. When Christians became the persecuting power they proved to be as equally power-hungry and intolerant as their erstwhile oppressors. However, equating loyalty to the state to loyalty to a deity isn't

---

[112] Gorski, Philip S. *Civil Religion Today*, pg. 2

something that is endemic to theocratic societies.

The "Cults of Personality" in Communism and Fascism exemplify a deity-less system that puts in place of a deity human leaders of a political movement. Christianity should learn from the history of these very oppressive regimes and instead of seeking to establish an ostensibly "Christian" civil religion which would prove to be no better than the secular atheist communists they seek to oppose, they should work towards religious freedom for all, the atheist, Wiccan, and even Satanist included. For those Christians who would be aghast at this suggestion, consider for once that the proper Christian methods of countering these belief (and unbelief) systems of thought are not civil, but spiritual. Reason with the discourse of words, not with the machinery of the state.

Another folly of worldly Christian Nationalism is the exclusion of Christians of other nations, tongues, and peoples. Once we establish a country like America as a "Christian" nation, inevitably comes the argument that we are a better Christian nation than others, and everyone else is somehow of a lesser strain. Political competition will be the result. While competition is almost the "name-of-the-game" when it comes to politics, it isn't when it comes to Christianity. When it comes to the Gospel, it's about the salvation of souls, not a worldly mud-slinging competition.

"For I say, through the grace given to me, to everyone who is among you, not to think of himself more highly than he ought to think, but to think soberly, as God has dealt to each one a measure of faith."[113]

God's people are comprised of citizens of many different nations throughout the world. The true Christian Nation above, Heaven, will have individuals with all sorts of backgrounds, skin, hair, and eye color and earthly nationalities. But all will acknowledge the name of Christ. People from all continents, whether it be the Americas, Europe, Asia, Africa and Australia are part of the true "Christian Nation", and this Nation, while comprised of people redeemed from this world, is most certainly *not of this world.*

"After these things I looked, and behold, a great multitude which no one could number, of all nations, tribes, peoples, and tongues, standing before the throne and before the Lamb, clothed with white robes, with palm branches in their hands, and crying out with a loud voice, saying, 'Salvation belongs to our God who sits on the throne, and

---

[113] Romans 12:3, *New King James Version*

to the Lamb!"[114]

[114] Revelation 7:9-10, *New King James Version*

CHAPTER NINE

The Clash of Cultures

THERE IS NO DOUBT ABOUT the clash of cultures within American society today. Politically it is seen as a conflict between traditional conservatives and progressive liberals and everyone in between. These political cultures drive our politics today and shift our nation between one extreme to the other in a seemingly non-stop pendulum effect. At the time of this writing we had the progression of two terms of a conservative President, George W. Bush, two terms of a liberal President, Barack Obama, and then the administration of Donald J. Trump, who was elected on the shoulders of a largely

Evangelical electorate.

There is no question that the clash of cultures in American society today is largely driven by religious preferences. There is also profound evidence that the political divide in the United States is informed by religion, and that religion being Christianity, especially the conservative stripe. A Pew Research poll back in 2006 indicated a growing support for the Republican Party among white evangelical voters.[115] Former President George W. Bush was elected on the strength of this political base on two consecutive terms.

The resurgence of the liberals helped paved the way for two terms under the Barack Obama administration. The Obama administration alienated many on the conservative Right, and in 2016, the Republican presidential contender, Donald J. Trump won an electoral victory over former First Lady and Secretary of State Hillary Clinton. This came as a shock to many, as most major news networks had predicted an overwhelming defeat for Trump. It was an upset of huge proportions.

---

[115] Rosentiel, Tom; Keeter, Scott. "Evangelicals and the GOP: An Update - Strongly Republican Group Not Immune to Party's Troubles", *Pew Research*, 18 October 2006

<https://www.pewresearch.org/2006/10/18/evangelicals-and-the-gop-an-update/> Accessed 12 August 2019.

It is possible that Trump's election came as a conservative reaction to the liberal policies of Obama. According to John Fea, author of *Believe Me: The Evangelical Road to Donald Trump*, White Evangelicals comprised 26% of the American voting bloc in the 2016 US Presidential Elections, and a staggering 81% of them voted for Trump. Fea, who himself is an Evangelical Christian, struggles to explain the phenomenon of how an admitted philanderer and a billionaire with little interest in Christianity except to fire up his electoral base, was able to galvanize a nation to elect him as President. Fea laments,

> *"Prior to his decision to run for office, very few Americans, including American evangelicals, were even aware that [Trump] was anything but a profane man-a playboy and adulterer who worshiped, not at the throne of God, but at the throne of Mammon".[116]*

After two terms of a progressive administration, conservative America was searching for a savior to reclaim the moral legacy of a nation; it wasn't important whether the Head of State was himself a moral person, but that he would give

---

[116] Fea, John. *Believe Me: The Evangelical Road to Donald Trump*, pg. 6.

them the political power that they needed to "make America great again". My fellow Christian and historian Fea concludes,

"Evangelicals claim to follow a Savior who relinquished worldly power-even to the point of giving His life. Yet they continue to place their hope in political candidates as a means of advancing an agenda that confuses the kingdom of God with the United States of America."[117]

It is a somber thought. Conscientious students of history, at least those not suffering from HPRS, will remember the painful lessons of the past, and, as Fea and myself are appealing, we should resist the temptation to repeat the mistakes of the past. Doing so could grow issues to proportions beyond our control and into something we had never intended for it to be. Could we perhaps be in danger of endorsing a so-called "lesser evil" to counteract a culture we feel is too secular, godless, and unfriendly to our faith? If so, we have lacked faith in God, and as such, we can no longer expect His blessing upon us as Christians.

Yes, to the conservative Christian the tide of growing secularism is alarming. The progressive culture grows bolder

---

[117] *Ibid.,* pg. 12.

and seeks to overrun every principle conservative and fundamental Christians believe to be essential in a godly nation. The Biblical view on human sexuality and the sanctity of life even before birth is being undermined by extreme social progressives. But as already shown so far throughout the bulk of this book so far, the answer isn't found in an overhaul of secular legislation, especially since not every individual lawmaker holds the same principles as another, and also because our Constitution forbids the state establishment of religion.

What is the answer to the growing un-Christian culture rising in America today? How are we to counter these anti-Christian trends? Well, what trends exactly, are we concerned about? Prayers in public school? The cultural battle over the acceptance of homosexuality? Abortion? Immigration reform? How to deal with Islamic radicalism? These are some of the most prominent social and moral issues surrounding American politics in the early decades of the 21st century.

In this volume we have continued to point out the pitfalls of pursuing a church-state union to any degree, slight or large, a concept which is both against the principles of Scripture and the Constitution of the United States of America. Now the sincere, morality loving, earnest Christian believer wonders how in the world to conquer the growing secular trends, and the solution is found in the methods of Jesus Christ Himself.

The Savior was frequently found in the midst of growing throngs of followers with ailments both physical and spiritual. He healed the sick, gave sight to the blind, and preached the Kingdom of Heaven to all who would listen. It is appropriate to repeat that never do we find Christ barging into government halls, lobbying government officials to create laws forbidding gay marriage or establishing a day of formal worship. No, the gentle and meek King of Kings sat under the shade of trees with gathering crowds, preaching, not a political speech to rile followers against their Roman oppressors; He came to save sinners and invited them to His Kingdom, one that wasn't found on this Earth.

The moral issues that plague the land must be met with a wise and Biblical approach, one that follows the admonitions of Scripture and respects the boundaries set by our civil Constitution. The only way this balance can be achieved is by taking advantage of the free marketplace of ideas, made possible by our Constitution which guarantees free speech and free exercise of religion. If we really want Christian morality to prevail as the nationwide norm, it must be done so not on the force of civil law, but by the free-will implementation of spiritual law in the hearts of individuals as we saw in our earlier discussion on the principles of the New Covenant.

If we are true New Covenant Christians, we must apply the covenantal promise of God who said,

"I will put my law in their inward parts, and write it in their hearts; and will be their God, and they shall be my people."[118]

Involving ourselves as Christians in the cultural and political divide only frustrates the New Covenant principle of looking forward to a Kingdom *not of this world*. By placing a civil authority to arbitrate spiritual matters, we put an idol in the place of God. Sure, the intention may be good; God seeks a people firm to principle and truth. However, in doing this we are applying worldly tactics to an otherwise spiritual fight, we become outmatched against our spiritual adversary, the Devil, who has had over six thousand years of experience.

The point of a Christian's obedience to God's moral Law now is not to establish an Earthly kingdom; to the contrary, the point of it is to prepare us for a Kingdom above. We are not called to be "minor judges", setting ourselves to determine the eligibility of people on Earth to be citizens of a

---

[118] Jeremiah 31:33, *King James Version*

country, heavenly or not, by the moral standards they choose to exercise. If they commit no civil crime, civil justices cannot indict them. Nor are we called to be executioners, meting out punishment to those that happen to hold different moral standards than ourselves. Jesus Himself had a few choice words to say about this.

"Judge not, that ye be not judged. For with what judgment ye judge, ye shall be judged: and with what measure ye mete, it shall be measured to you again. And why beholdest thou the mote that is in thy brother's eye, but considerest not the beam that is in thine own eye?"[119]

Here it is very clear we are not fit to be judges of our fellow man. No civil magistrate can mete out godly justice. Sure, we are to determine right and wrong by what is revealed in the Word of God; but judging is the work of God who can see not just the outward appearance and actions of man, but also his thoughts, intentions and motivations. To determine the inner motives of others is not something we can ever hope to accomplish, and something we should never try. This is why we cannot win a world to Christ by embracing a political

---

[119] Matthew 7:1-3, *King James Version*

identity. Forming civil policies around our religious convictions only incite ire in those that do not share our convictions. Encouraging a political divide based on religion will certainly backfire on Christians. We will be no better than the Pharisees of Christ's day.

As Christians that hold that God's Word is transcendent from God and true, we take seriously its moral claims. But in the New Covenant, the moral standards of God's Law are not something we are to make others do. It is for those of us who believe that are expected to comply. We would detest having atheism forced upon us in a Communist country; we would loathe to have sharia law apply to us in a Muslim country, or our Christianity discriminated against in a Hindu nation. So then why legally coerce people to follow "Judeo-Christian" principles in a so-called "Christian nation"? Are we not to follow the words of Jesus when He said,

"And as ye would that men should do to you, do ye also to them likewise."[120]

Christianity stands unique among those above-mentioned religious (and irreligious) ideologies as we believe

---

[120] Luke 6:31, *King James Version*

in a country out of this world. We do not seek to make others conform to our standards because we would not appreciate having the same done to us.

Therefore, in the clash of cultures we see today and, in every generation, before and in the future, we must avoid the almost irresistible urge to resort to political solutions to the moral and spiritual woes that seem to threaten to tear the fabric of society. Are there exceptions? Perhaps. We will elaborate in the next chapter about the Biblical admonition to respect civil authority. There is a difference between the civil and moral spheres of Caesar and God respectively, and how we can affect a balance for the good without trampling upon the consciences of those that hold different religious convictions.

Turning the legislature of the United States of America into the Sanhedrin 2.0 would be a disaster. America is not the Israel of ancient times, nor do we hope for it to ever be. That Israel still had the favor of God, and as God's people they were to bring the light of truth to all the nations around them. But they fell repeatedly into apostasy, clamored to have a worldly king rule over them, kings who, more often than not, led the people to worship false gods and finally caused Israel and Judah to fall into exile and obscurity.

Not understanding the New Covenant, the Sanhedrin of the New Testament called for the crucifixion of the Messiah.

Collaborating with the Roman State in the most egregious case of Church and State union in history, this woeful combination resulted in the murder of God's Only Begotten Son. Should we expect any Church and State collaboration to do any better?

May this plea not fall on deaf ears or blind eyes. Christians, Christians. It is not our duty to make America "Christian" again, but to make Christians of all who are willing in America, and in the world at large. By word and example, we can counter the growing tide of secularist culture and irreligiousness. For even if a small minority should accept basic Christian truths and practice them in their lives, on the strength of their convictions and faith in God, all the host of Hell cannot stand against them.

The example of a godly life in a Christian would do more wonders in witnessing for Christ than a plethora of "Judeo-Christian" based laws in the books of civil legislature. One thing is for sure, it would be a more powerful witness. In this independent, individualized Western culture, people are more likely to follow an example than raw legal dictates.

Enforcing civil laws would only serve to actuate outward behavior, and not change a person's conviction one bit. Imagine the devout Christian in an Islamic nation, forced to adhere to sharia law. If he is true to his conviction, he will only obey outward sharia laws that do not violate his conscience; if he is forced to conform to any statutes that require him to reject any portion of his Christian beliefs, he will more than likely resist and welcome death rather than give up his faith. Would it be any different if the situation were switched? The rule of an Islamic theocracy a Christian should never accept. However, the answer to an Islamic theocracy isn't to replace it with a Christian one. The answer is to maintain a society of civil religious freedom, for the Christian, the Muslim, the Jew, the Hindu, the Buddhist, the atheist, the Wiccan, and even the Satanist.

God does not need the help of civil governments to defend Himself. He is quite capable of defending Himself. When imperfect people try to defend God, the defense is liable to be marred with mistakes, human misjudgments, and the tendency for the defenders to be full of themselves than of Him whom they are defending. When this happens, the cause of God is ruined, and more people are repulsed from, instead of driven to, the Cross.

If this cautioning is not enough, perhaps the words of Christ Himself would jolt us from a dreadful hangover after being drunk with the wine of mixing together the holy and the worldly:

"Woe unto thee, Chorazin! woe unto thee, Bethsaida! for

if the mighty works, which were done in you, had been done in Tyre and Sidon, they would have repented long ago in sackcloth and ashes. But I say unto you, It shall be more tolerable for Tyre and Sidon at the day of judgment, than for you. And thou, Capernaum, which art exalted unto heaven, shalt be brought down to hell: for if the mighty works, which have been done in thee, had been done in Sodom, it would have remained until this day. But I say unto you, That it shall be more tolerable for the land of Sodom in the day of judgment, than for thee."[121]

What a frightening and sobering warning! That Chorazin, which is a short distance away from Bethsaida and Capernaum, a set of towns that held the Abrahamic faith would be described as less than "tolerable" in the day of judgment than Sodom shows us how serious God is on those that have claimed to follow Him, but are worse than the Sodomites. These cities would suffer even more than Sodom during the punitive measures meted out during the judgments of God because they are more accountable for the knowledge of God they claim to have, but yet have proven to be no better.

Christians receive no spiritual benefit from demonizing

---

[121] Matthew 11:21-24, *King James Version*

an opposing political group. The Apostle Paul's earnest appeal was that everyone, not merely those we wish to see as wicked, but ourselves as well, see the utter need we have for a Savior. He wrote,

"This is a faithful saying, and worthy of all acceptation, that Christ Jesus came into the world to save sinners; of whom I am chief."[122]

All have sinned, and all are in need of a Savior. Liberal, Conservative, Moderate alike, need the wonderful grace of Christ. Democrats, Republicans, Libertarians, and Independents. Individuals will inevitably have their political preferences, but in the sight of God we must remember we are all sinners alike. It is better to bear the badge of Jesus Christ than to hold any political party affiliation.

Perhaps you are not voting to instill Christian values on others, but rather to preserve the Christian culture of America. Ask yourself, how important is this? Does culture save people? Or does a personal acceptance of Jesus as Lord and Savior do that? This society can end up being as atheistic and as secular as possible, but should opposing it in politics be the priority of

---

[122] 1 Timothy 1:15, *King James Version*

the Christian? Or should the living and sharing of the Gospel?

CHAPTER TEN

The Powers That Be

UNDERSTANDING THE BIBLICAL ROLE of a secular government is not too difficult. First, we will need to outline the different types of government outlined in the Biblical testimony. From the discussions within the previous chapters, we can easily identify at least three:

1. God's Universal Government
2. God's Theocracy on Earth
3. Civil and Secular Government

With the first, we define God's Universal Government as God's rulership over the entire universe. This is God's governance over every created being and thing. We recognize God as the source of all Laws governing the universe, Moral, Physical and Spiritual. The Law of Gravity, for example, is a Physical Law. Without it, the universe would be in complete disarray. So essential is the Law of Gravity for the physical order of the universe that the famed physicist, the late Stephen Hawking wrote,

"Because there is a law such as gravity, the universe can and will create itself from nothing."[123]

Here, Hawking has attempted to reason that a Cosmic Designer is not necessary to explain the existence of everything because gravity can account for the order and life we witness around us today. However, the brute assumption of the existence of the Law of Gravity begs the question, where did such laws of order originate? Even if gravity were to explain the appearance of design and order we see in the universe, its existence cannot be merely assumed, it requires an origin.

---

[123] Quoted by Dacey, James. "Talking Hawking and God", *Physics World*, 3 September 2010, <**https://physicsworld.com/a/talking-hawking-and-god/**> Accessed 17 June 2019.

The Christian assumes that the Author and Designer of the Laws governing the universe is God. For the Christian, this supplies the answer to the philosophical question of existence and meaning. It grounds transcendent moral laws in objectivity and provides a compass in times where there is a need for moral clarity.

Because God's jurisdiction includes everything and everyone, we know the moral laws that govern one part of the universe apply to all parts. There is a standard of goodness and righteousness, the boundaries of which are denoted by God's moral laws. If those laws are violated, the boundaries are crossed, and the consequences are the inevitable result. Paul writes succinctly,

"For the wages of sin is death..."[124]

The consequence of sinning is death, pain, and suffering. The Bible is very clear on this point. This is why there is the Gospel, the need of every human on this planet for a Savior, and the good news that if they believe in Him, they could attain eternal life. The Fall of Man required for there to be a plan of salvation to rescue humanity from the chains and

---

[124] Romans 6:23, *King James Version*

consequences of the sins they have fallen into. There was a legal debt to be paid, and God's Son was sent to pay it on our behalf.

The second type of Biblical government is God's theocracy on Earth. Before the Son of God being incarnated as the living Word on this Earth, God established the theocracy of ancient Israel, bestowing a sacred covenant upon the descendants of Abraham, promising them the inheritance of the nations of the Earth should they remain faithful to His statutes forever. The theocracy was contingent upon Israel fulfilling its divine mandate, which we saw in chapters six and seven as being largely unfulfilled. However, it was intended to last forever, and it would have, had Israel continued to obey the covenant God made with them. The penchant of the Israelites to rely on human instead of divine strength caused their downfall.

The Earthly theocratic experiment failed, not because God failed, but because humans failed by accepting worldly leaders and practicing wickedness. The biblical example in-and-of-itself should already be a warning to anyone today and in the future the futility of establishing a theocratic or semi-theocratic government, no matter how noble the intentions may be. If ancient Israel could botch their moment with the very presence of God in their midst, how much more today with presumptive Christian theocrats, who do not have any way to directly consult with God?

The third type of Biblical government is the civil and secular government. Defined by Christ as "the things that are Caesar's",[125] the secular government stands in contrast to the theocracy God-ordained. Because Israel failed to abide by its covenant with God, He would allow nations to rule over them with governments that did not recognize or know Him. In the case of Judah, the mighty Babylonian Empire would rule over God's people for several decades. While the Babylonians were certainly not without their share of gods such as Marduk, the patron god of the city of Babylon, their rulership over Judah wasn't considered theocratic, it was secular. As a multicultural empire the Babylonians allowed the Jews (for the most part, except for that bit described in Daniel chapter 3) and other peoples the liberty to worship their deities.

The subsequent empires that ruled over Judea had a similar stance regarding religious freedom with the Persians tossing the devoted Daniel into a den of lions, the would-be genocide of the Jews during the time of Queen Esther. The Hellenistic Empire contributed their share of religious persecution during the Seleucid rule of the Judean province.

---

[125] Matthew 22:21, *King James Version*

Antiochus IV Epiphanes, the Seleucid king decreed the forbidding of Jewish religious practices, resulting in the Maccabean revolt in the 2nd century BCE.

The rule of Rome brought its own edition of religious suppression throughout its dominance of several centuries. As the Christian Church struggled to grow, the Pagan Roman Empire found itself at odds with the new religious sect. A conflict was inevitable, and persecution was the result, as pointed out in the first few chapters of this volume. The consequences of apostasy were burdensome on the Judeans. They would never again have full and complete autonomy from foreign meddling, and a true theocracy in the mold of the Davidic Kingdom would no longer be an option. The people of God, both literal and spiritual Israel would be under the yolk of worldly civil oppressors; hence the New Testament promise of the "blessed hope"[126] which Paul writes is "the glorious appearing of the great God and our Saviour Jesus Christ".

With these definitions in mind, we must now analyze the essential differences, and how to apply the Biblical principles to our situation today. This is imperative, given our mandate to

---

[126] Titus 2:13, *King James Version*

The Gospel commission is to *teach*, not *coerce*, all nations to come to the knowledge of Christ, and hopefully submit themselves to the King of Kings.

According to the Christian worldview, government #1, the government administered by God Almighty is the overall governing entity in the universe. This means that God is sovereign and supreme above all things and all beings. He is all-knowing and omnipotent. Nothing happens in the universe without His knowledge, from the grandest supernova or the movement of the tiniest speck of dust on this forlorn planet. We can call this administration, the sphere of "universal government", simply UG.

Government #2 is the "Earthly Theocracy", or ET. This is God's government on Earth, administered by human authorities under the direct guidance of God. This best describes the system under which ancient Israel operated, and under which the Old Covenant was administered.

Government #3 is man led civil government, or CG. This is the system under which we operate today. After the passing of the Old Covenant and the ET, believers find

---

[127] Matthew 28:19, *King James Version*

themselves under CG, but are always recognizing they are still under God's UG, which we recognize as our higher authority. The Apostle Peter reminds us that we need to respect our Earthly authorities in their jurisdiction:

"Submit yourselves to every ordinance of man for the Lord's sake: whether it be to the king, as supreme; Or unto governors, as unto them that are sent by him for the punishment of evildoers, and for the praise of them that do well."[128]

This illustrates how the Christian's relationship to CG should be. There is no record of any disciples or members of the early Church opposing Earthly authorities just because they didn't like them. Whether the administration is liberal, conservative or libertarian, Democrat, Republican, we must submit to ordinances that do not violate our basic consciences. Even under very difficult administrations, we are to keep our cool and show ourselves to be model citizens, and only protesting and disobeying ordinances that violate our beliefs. The same Peter remarked at Pentecost,

---

[128] 1 Peter 2:13-14, *King James Version*

"We ought to obey God rather than men."[129]

In dealing with CG, the Scriptures maintain a wonderful balance, teaching Christians to exemplify model citizenship but at the same keeping them faithful to a Higher Power and focused on the Kingdom "not of this world", God's UG. This is why it is essential for us Christians to strive for religious liberty, not just for themselves, but for others as well. We recognize each individual's conscience as sacred, and in the interest of furthering the Gospel, we treat others just as how we would like to be treated.

The Scriptures do not coerce anyone of a different conviction to hold to Christian truths. The work of changing hearts belongs to the Holy Spirit. We must not coerce atheists to accept that homosexuality is immoral, or Muslims to take civil oaths with their hands on top of a Bible. We cannot, by the machinery of CG, enforce the standards of the UG for they are different spheres of governance, different jurisdictions.

But what of the passage that states

"Let every soul be subject unto the higher powers. For there is no power but of God: the powers that be are

---

129 Acts 5:29, *King James Version*

ordained of God"?

This text is from Romans 13:1, KJV. It is often used to support Christian influence in CG. In 2018, Attorney General Jeff Sessions, serving the Trump Administration and in defense of the strict immigration policy of that administration stated,

"I would cite you to the Apostle Paul and his clear and wise command in Romans 13 to obey the laws of the government because God has ordained the government for his purposes…Orderly and lawful processes are good in themselves. Consistent, fair application of law is in itself a good and moral thing and that protects the weak, it protects the lawful. Our policies that can result in short-term separation of families are not unusual or unjustified."[130]

A worried columnist aptly observed,

"Romans 13 has been cited by Nazi sympathizers and apartheid-enforcers, slave owners and loyalists opposed to

---

[130] Quoted by Topan, Kal. "Sessions cites Bible to defend immigration policies resulting in family separations", *CNN*, 14 June 2018

<https://edition.cnn.com/2018/06/14/politics/jeff-sessions-immigration-policy-defense-biblical/index.html> Accessed 19 June 2019.

the American Revolution. Modern Christians have wrestled with how to apply the passage to issues like abortion, same-sex marriage and taxes."[131]

This is a serious issue, folks. Certain lawmakers in CG's have used this passage to appeal to Christian audiences everywhere to keep them loyal to the state regardless of the policies enacted. And because many Christians do not take the time to analyze exactly what the Bible is saying here, they will be deceived. The passage is certainly not endorsing full compliance to CG at all times. Nor is it suggesting that the state should be made Christian, so the Christian citizen would have no qualms following its mandates.

The main thing to consider is that the CG in authority at the time of the writing of Paul's letter to the Romans was none other than the Roman Empire, a pagan political power that had no allegiance to the God of Heaven. This same government would, in the span of the next couple of centuries cause the deaths of thousands of Christians and encourage in their citizens the mass persecution and discrimination of the same.

---

[131] Burke, Daniel. "What does the Bible verse Jeff Sessions quoted really mean?", CNN, 15 June 2018

<https://edition.cnn.com/2018/06/15/us/sessions-bible-quote-apostle-paul/index.html> Accessed 19 June 2019.

As we saw towards the end of chapter 8, during the Roman Imperial era, before the official designation of Christianity as the state religion, it is well known that the state required its citizens to pay homage to the Roman deities as a means of showing loyalty to the Roman state. Refusal to do so was tantamount to treason. Of course, by principle, Christians could not fulfill this requirement. They stood firm by their convictions that only God could accept their worship, and in such a situation they exercised their prerogative to obey God's UG over man's CG.

Because of this, the body of Christian believers were subjected to all sorts of mistreatment and even death, since treason was a capital offense. Government officials and common citizens alike, took the opportunity to ridicule, attack, and kill these individuals who they believed were disloyal to their government. And yet, Paul saw fit to appeal to believers to submit themselves to such an authority in the areas they could conscientiously do so. Many things needed to change in that corrupt, infidel, and despotic Roman Imperial government.

However, we do not see the Apostles nor any of the early Christians pushing for a change in the Imperial government to have civil laws reflect Christian values. Indeed, we do not even see an armed Christian uprising in revolt against their Roman oppressors as we saw with the Jewish

Maccabean revolt against the Seleucids. We have not an inkling of support for civil violence against a despotic civil power anywhere in the New Testament. Instead, we see entreaties towards repaying evil with kindness.

North American Christians today tend to have a different perspective on things, thanks to Christian Nationalistic fervor, a mingling of traditional Christian moral values, Patriotic zeal and desire for political power, a perfect example of mixing the holy and the profane. The American caricature of the conservative Christian has become one of a Bible-wielding, gun-toting and flag displaying[132] individual instead of a Stephen, who, on the verge of being stoned for his faith, did not even so much as raise a fist against his oppressors but rather looked up for his hope of a life to come.

This image of a power-hungry, arms obsessed, ostensibly patriotic American Christian is not only damaging to America, but it is also damaging to Christianity. It harkens back to the days of the Crusader attempts to take back the Holy Land, igniting a Holy War between Christianity and Islam, only that the armored Knight wearing the Cross insignia is

---

[132] Kuruvilla, Carol. "West Virginia mom sparks backlash for posing on Twitter with Bible, gun, and American flag", *New York Daily News*, 10 July 2014.

<https://www.nydailynews.com/news/national/conservative-mom-poses-bible-gun-flag-article-1.1862261> Accessed 22 August 2019.

replaced with the flag-draped citizen with an AR-15 in one hand and a Bible in the other. This is an indication of the failure of the Gospel in this part of the world; that God needs armed knights to propagate the Kingdom of Heaven shows a lack of both faith and practical logic.

This book is not a critique of the Gun lobby or the Second Amendment. It is an American right to bear arms as it is an American right to have freedom of religion. However, this book will not hold back in expressing the utter disappointment and disgust that conservative Christians who claim to represent Christ have allowed this image of a Christian American Nationalist to persist, thanks to their preferences for the political Right, and in essence, have sought to instill their brand of religion upon the Nation.

Conservative Christians today have lost sight of the true UG of God and have attempted to co-opt the Biblical purpose of the CG which God had already designated for a particular purpose, and instead have envisioned a semi-ET, one that seeks to give substantial favor and preferences to Judeo-Christianity. This is especially what the Founding Fathers of America sought to avoid, as we saw in chapters four and five. "Free exercise of religion" isn't a euphemism for "free exercise of religion for us Christians only". It means what it means; no "if's", "and's", "but's" and "or's". Free exercise of religion for all.

This is why American Christians if they are truly faithful to the principles of the United States Constitution, should not have been up in political arms when homosexual marriage was legalized in the *Obergefell v. Hodges* US Supreme Court decision in 2015. As long as Christian ministers themselves (along with their Jewish and Muslim counterparts) have the option of freely exercising their religious right to decline to perform such unions should it violate their religious conscience, there is nothing to fear. Paul admonished civil obedience to the CG of Imperial Rome in all areas which did not violate their loyalty and obligation towards God and encouraged no Christian incursions upon her political operation.

The legalization of gay marriage in America is not an edict requiring Christians to violate their loyalty to God. It merely means for those who have no personal qualms against homosexual marriage, they have that option. It is a win for religious liberty because more convictions can be accommodated by civil authority. This is exactly what liberty is. We may not like to implications of the outcome of the decision, and we may personally be against the practice of homosexual marriage, but unless the law dictates that we must personally violate our conscience, this is a victory for true religious freedom. People with convictions that do not frown upon homosexual unions can now exercise those convictions.

If we worry about how this starts up a moral slippery slope and that it would be that much more difficult to convert a world spiraling into moral disaster, we must then step-up and place our efforts, not in political opposition, but in personal ministry. Reveal the love of God, and how He can transform lives. Win others by the witness of a godly life, personal witness, and Christ-like compassion, not by creating laws to coerce them to conform to your views. Just like how you would not appreciate Islamic Sharia laws being imposed upon you, treat others, even those whom you disagree with, as you wish to be treated. Christians are to seek true liberty for the soul for everyone, so that as Christ said,

> *"Whosoever will come after me, let him deny himself, and take up his cross, and follow me."[133]*

The Scriptures enjoin no legal forcing of non-Christians to conform to Christian morality. You will not find one New Covenant text to suggest this. But what of Romans 13 then? When it says:

---

[133] Mark 8:34, *King James Version*

"For rulers are not a terror to good works, but to the evil. Wilt thou then not be afraid of the power? do that which is good, and thou shalt have praise of the same: For he is the minister of God to thee for good. But if thou do that which is evil, be afraid; for he beareth not the sword in vain: for he is the minister of God, a revenger to execute wrath upon him that doeth evil".?[134]

Since Paul wrote this while Christian believers were under the civil authority of Rome, we can garner several principles from this very passage and what it means for us today. Here are the major points to take away:

1. **Civil governments are ordained of God.**
   - This does not mean God approves the methods or laws of these governments, but it does mean they serve a purpose in God's overall will. God gives every CG that has exited their chance under the sun. If they prove to be evil regimes, God also arranges for their downfall. "…he removeth

---

134 Romans 13:3-4, *King James Version*

kings, and setteth up kings…"[135] God allows governments of all types to arise, since governments serve a purpose of establishing law and order, and they keep society from falling into chaos. However, He brings the wicked ones to destruction, such as seen in the downfall of Nazi Germany and most of the Communist regimes that arose after the dawn of the 20th century.

2. **The law enforcement branches of these governments are to be respected.**

- They may not always do things perfectly, and many law enforcement organizations are in dire need of reform, it behooves the Christian to always be respectful to the rule of law. If a law violates their Christian conscience, then the believer is expected to place a priority on God's Higher Law. Police and Military bear not the sword "in vain", but maintain local civil and international order respectively.

3. **The "evil" referred to in this text is civil lawlessness.**

- Jesus quantified a divide in the jurisdictions of Caesar and God, "Render therefore unto

---

[135] Daniel 2:21, *King James Version*

Caesar the things which are Caesar's; and unto God the things that are God's".[136] Christ made it clear the spheres of governance have separate functions; Caesar was expected to rule and keep civil order, such as prohibiting murder, stealing, and maiming under pain of civil punitive measures. God is accepted as ruling all things, with Caesar acting not as His direct agent, but as an unwitting ruler under God's greater rule. Paul was cognizant that the government of pagan Rome could not entirely reflect the moral framework of God's government, but at least they could maintain civil order.

Now that we have established the basic meaning of the text in the context of the time it was written, we can apply its principles to our situation today. First, we must eliminate the thinking that we must make our civil government conform to Christian standards. The bulk of this volume has been dedicated to pointing out the practical and spiritual pitfalls of such an endeavor. It is worth repeating that we see no example

---

[136] Matthew 22:21, *King James Version*

in Scripture of Christ, His disciples, or the Early Church attempting to effect changes in civil law to conform to Christian standards. Therefore, the United States government falls under the 3rd definition of Biblical government. It is not reflective of UG, nor is it an ET.

Second, while the Scriptures command obedience to Earthly governments, we should render obedience only to laws that do not violate our Christian conscience. A historical American example that deals with this situation is the Fugitive Slave Act of 1850, passed by the United States Congress. The Act required citizens to report and return slaves escaping their masters in the South. Northern Christians, many of whom were staunch abolitionists, openly defied this law. The Abolitionist Christians regarded no man as the property of another, and it violated their conscience to return a slave to his master. In this case, the Christian would be expected to refuse to obey such an unjust law and accept any civil consequences that would follow. The Fugitive Slave Act required the Christian to commit an act of commission, which is to actively send a slave back to his master. Thankfully, that horrid Act was overturned in June of 1864, and rightfully called a "blood-red stain" on the "statute book of the Republic" and deserved to be "wiped out forever".[137]

Thirdly, there must be a defining line between that which is moral and that which is civil. Morality, in order to have the power of objectivity, has to be considered as transcendent, derived from a Divine Lawmaker. There is subjective morality, one which is defined by man, but because it can easily change as quickly as the wind blows, its foundation is weak. Biblical morality is founded upon God's Word and is immutable and transcendently objective. It is divine and thus cannot be administered by mere fallible humans. Civil refers to our relationship with one another. Being "civil" to each other requires us to treat each other with respect and in peace. Being "uncivil" causes disorder and brings chaos, and therefore can be administered by human authorities because these are common sense statutes that are empirically shown to keep the peace and promote order in society. The protection of an individual's right to life, property, and the pursuit of happiness is a civil matter and their handling by Earthly rulers and judges can be expected. Can the moral and the civil overlap? Certainly, and they often do. The Moral Decalogue contains commandments to not kill, steal or bear

---

[137] Fehrenbacher, Don E. *The Slaveholding Republic: An Account of the United States Government's Relations to Slavery*, pg. 250.

false witness. These are also civil concerns. But while coveteousness is a moral issue, it is not something a civil authority should handle for it involves an act of the mind, and only the Creator of the universe can read the minds of men.

This is crucial in our understanding of how religious liberty should work. Learning to know the difference between what is properly moral, what is civil, and the areas which overlap will help us in our approach to the relationship between God's UG and man's CG. The abolition of slavery is both a moral and a civil issue. Assuming ownership of another human being will cause social and civil disorder. It is also moral in that God commanded "Thou shalt not steal" and enslaving another man means stealing his freedom and God's claim upon him. Murder is both uncivil and immoral, and considered wrong in many legal traditions within and outside of Judeo-Christianity. Nazi Germany clearly went way beyond the civil and the moral when their implementation of the Final Solution made them uncivilized, murderous brutes.

In the following chart, we see the dichotomy between morality and civility, how each must be administered, and what the essential difference should be between the two, and in what areas they overlap. A civil government is not wholly divested from moral concerns, but its moral concerns are only to be confined where they overlap with civil concerns.

Moral Law	Civil Law
Church	State
God's Rulership	Caesar's Rulership
Deals with our moral obligation to God and our fellow man	Deals with our civil obligation to our fellow man
From a Transcendent Lawmaker	From Human lawmakers
Objective and Immutable	Subjective and liable to changes
Defines Sin	Defines Crimes and Misdemeanors
Governs the Universe	Governs the Civil State

Here we see that there is some overlap between the moral and the civil, as laws against stealing and murder are moral and civil. However, you cannot expect a civil government to prosecute coveteousness as required by the tenth commandment in the Biblical Moral Decalogue. Therefore, this would lie under the purview of a moral code that is impossible to apply to civil code! Imagine the US government making advertisement illegal since it encourages coveteousness! Oh, how the small-government political conservatives would be up-in-arms, protesting the government overreach, affecting the free market. Fortunately, morality is what we render to God, and civility is what we render to each other for the sake of keeping peace and order. Civility is something that someone of any religious conviction, or lack of it, can apply without violating their consciences, however with morality, more nuance is needed to ensure all convictions are accommodated. Besides, even atheists, Buddhists, Muslims, Jews, Hindus, and many other religious and non-religious convictions would agree that murder and stealing are wrong. The problem arises where concepts of morality begin to vary between religious beliefs, and it may be tricky to determine what issues exactly are within the purview of the civil state to decide.

Abortion is one of the most hotly debated subjects in American politics and plays a huge part in the political divide between the two major political parties today. For conservatives, Abortion is murder of the unborn; for progressives abortion should be a right since women should be allowed to make their own decisions about their body and not the government. This is a moral issue in all cases and contingently civil based upon how society sees the unborn.

Should unborn babies have rights? Are they even to be considered as people? Questions like these further fuel the debate and cause confusion. The simple answer should be, if the unborn are persons, then they need to be protected by law, and abortion would simply be murder by both moral and civil standards. But because the boundary at which life begins changes according to the opinions of men, there remains significant political debate over the practice. In the landmark decision *Roe v. Wade*, the SCOTUS implemented a trimester framework for which to allow government intervention in later trimesters, but not in the early ones. Ironically enough, the Pro-Life movement against abortion used to be a liberal political concern, and only after Roe did the conservatives take the pro-life cause to protest government overreach.[138]

Abortion is the interruption of the development of life and is therefore a moral issue. That it is a civil one will be determined how the sacredness of life is viewed by the civil realm, and where the public views the line between life and non-life. The Scriptures do state that God has His eye even upon the unborn,

"For thou hast possessed my reins: thou hast covered me

---

[138] Williams, Daniel K. "The Liberal Origins of the Pro-Life Movement", *Principles*,

<**https://www.getprinciples.com/the-liberal-origins-of-the-pro-life-movement/**> Accessed 10 August 2019.

in my mother's womb,"[139]

and referring to John the Baptist,

> *"For he shall be great in the sight of the Lord, and shall drink neither wine nor strong drink; and he shall be filled with the Holy Ghost, even from his mother's womb."[140]*

This shows the importance God places upon individuals even while they are in the womb of their mother. Unfortunately, because not everyone accepts the claims of the Bible to be the Word of God, not everyone can and will accept what it says about the sanctity of the life of the unborn. Because of the political volatility of the subject, the best way to save unborn lives is to bring people to the knowledge of the God of the Bible so they can accept its moral standards and claims to the sacredness of life, even of those in the womb.

Petitioning Capitol Hill to overturn *Roe v. Wade* is fruitless because not all of the governed accept the authority of the Bible. Once people accept the authority of God's Word, they may see abortion as murder, even without the civil

---

[139] Psalm 139:13, *King James Version*

[140] Luke 1:15, *King James Version*

government having to mandate it as such. This is the ideal situation.

The loyalty of Christians to God's UG will allow them to uphold Biblical morality without the need for a CG to legislate it. Indeed, the CG's purpose is to uphold civil order with civil laws, and to leave the religious consciences up to each individual. This is how we are to view the "powers that be" concerning the Christian faith.

Again, and again we implore, we must avoid the temptation to mingle Church and State. To succumb to that temptation would be quite frankly, un-Christian and un-American. We can do better than that, American Christians.

CHAPTER ELEVEN

A Summary and The Conclusion

WE HAVE NOW COME TO THE conclusion of this analysis on the importance of Religious Liberty in the context of Christianity and the American government. It has been a rough ride, but we've made it! Zipping through thousands of years of history, we've seen the Biblical and historical data that shows us that mingling Church and State is never a good idea, whether for the Church or the State.

Christ made it clear that His Kingdom is "not of this world". We have also seen egregious examples in history of Christian violations of religious freedom and it is appalling.

Until we solve this issue, we cannot expect to bring people to the foot of the Cross of Christ. By presuming God's stamp of approval on our political activities, we tend to repulse away from the Christian faith those who have a different political persuasion than ours. This is a disservice to Christianity.

With the whole world watching, Christians must walk in the way of Christ.

"He that saith he abideth in him ought himself also so to walk, even as he walked."[141]

Did Jesus walk to the seat of a legislature to lobby civil laws to enforce the precepts of His Kingdom? He did not. He spent His time gaining citizens for His Heavenly Kingdom. Did Jesus arm His followers and encouraged them to resist Roman rule? He did not. Malchus would have something to say about that. Did Jesus undermine the worldly civil authority of the pagan autocrat Caesar? He did not. In fact, He commanded His followers to pay tribute; yet many American Christian conservatives believe taxation is immoral. [142] Did Jesus

---

[141] 1 John 2:6, *King James Version*

[142] Stahl, Jason. *Right Moves: The Conservative Think Tank in American Political Culture since 1945*, pg. 115.

command His followers to rescue Him as He was led to the Governor Pontius Pilate? No, instead He declared to the Roman official,

"My kingdom is not of this world: if my kingdom were of this world, then would my servants fight, that I should not be delivered to the Jews: but now is my kingdom not from hence."[143]

And still, many Christians want to influence legislation to reflect their values without considering the cost of appealing to worldly power.

The list of instances where religious oppression has taken place is too long to include in this book. Religious oppression has taken place since the beginning of known history and will continue until the end of time. But this does not mean you need to take part in it. You can play a part in countering it. Let your voice and vote make a difference. Protest and vote against measures that threaten Religious Liberty for all. Remember, do unto others what you would have them do to you. Legislature favoring Christianity may actually be harming it. Heed the words of James Madison,

---

[143] John 18:36, *King James Version*

quoted before but which we can never quote enough,

> "religion [and government] will both exist in greater purity, the less they are mixed together."

The government should be out of the business of regulating issues of the religious conscience. So long as the matter can be settled without material injury to another individual, there shouldn't be any regulation. Remember the litmus test proposed by Thomas Jefferson,

> "But it does me no injury for my neighbour to say there are twenty gods, or no god. It neither picks my pocket nor breaks my leg."[144]

Jefferson knew the best way for truth to propagate is not through civil coercion, but by free inquiry and reason.

> "Reason and free enquiry are the only effectual agents against error. Give a loose to them, they will support the true religion, by bringing every false one to their tribunal, to the test of their investigation. They are the natural

---

[144] Jefferson, Thomas. *Notes on the State of Virginia*, pg. 170.

enemies of error, and of error only."[145]

Jefferson continues,

"Millions of innocent men, women, and children, since the introduction of Christianity, have been burnt, tortured, fined, imprisoned; yet we have not advanced one inch towards uniformity. What has been the effect of coercion? To make one half the world fools, and the other half hypocrites."[146]

Coercion only makes hypocrites of those who outwardly conform to avoid punishment, but yet do not truly believe in the validity of the ideology coerced upon them. If only the rank and file of conservative American Christians could take this to heart! What countless hours wasted in legal debates, in theological and political tirades could have been saved?

Apply the Jefferson litmus test to the issues. For example, on same-sex marriage, does someone with a homosexual lifestyle proverbially "pick your picket" or "break

---

[145] *Ibid.,* ppg. 170-171.

[146] *Ibid.,* pg. 172.

194

your leg"? If he keeps his business to himself without harming you in any tangible way, why would you legally coerce your fellow Americans to maintain God's ideal marriage between one man and one woman? God is more than capable of defending His intent on marriage. He does not need fallible American lawmakers and justices to do this for Him. Separate your Religion and the State.

If there is any skepticism on the validity of the American historical testimony on what the relation between Church and State should be, perhaps the testimony of the Holy Scriptures can convince the American Christian to abandon the folly of putting political measures in the place of living and sharing the Gospel. We should place the realms of God and Caesar into their respective spheres and honor their authority in the right places. God is ruler overall and is the Author of moral order but ordains imperfect human systems to uphold civil order and keep the peace between men.

In the first few chapters of the book, we saw how religious oppression and the escape from it have helped birth the colonies that would become our great nation. We have also seen how the oppressed became the oppressor and the irony of such a situation. Then we discussed other unfortunate events involving religious oppression in history leading up to that point and beyond.

After realizing the unnecessary suffering this has all caused, we analyzed the contributions of the Protestant Reformation, and how Luther pioneered the concept of separating the jurisdiction of the State from that of the Church into "two kingdoms". However not all Protestants went along with this ideology and were at times just as bad as the Inquisition in suppressing the religious consciences of Catholics and even their fellow Protestants throughout history. Thankfully, the ideology of separation of Church and State did not die and was picked up by key Enlightenment writers like John Locke to more fully expound upon the importance of religious liberty which in turn influenced the American Founders to form a similar ideology. Roger Williams and William Penn forged colonies which allowed the free exercise of religion for all, and the successes of these civil experiments encouraged lawmakers down the line to continue this practice until it was codified in our Bill of Rights once America became an independent nation.

The path to civil religious freedom has been riddled with bitter lessons, trial, and error. The reason why humanity has continued to propagate the pernicious attitude of religious oppression is partly due to HPRS, which is the inability, whether willingly or in ignorance, to remember the bitter lessons of past history and the consequences that arose when religious convictions were suppressed.

It has also been clear to us that the New Covenant has the Christian looking forward to a Heavenly home, not a worldly Christian community. The Old Covenant with its theocratic system of government is no more and replaced with a far better blessed hope. Since the New Covenant requires believers to accept Christ and have His Law written upon their hearts, there is no room to expect external civil laws denoting our moral obligations to God. God needs no human intermediary to administer His Laws.

Then we saw how the Old Covenant system, with its theocratic government was an agreement between ancient Israel and God, with God as its direct head of State, the same God who could read hearts and minds, and rule with precise and perfect justice. Along the way, Israel wanted to follow the pagan nations around them, and asked for a fallible, human Head of State. This, God allowed, but made it clear it was not His will, and that there were consequences to this move. Sure enough, as a consequence, Israel almost fell during the reign of their first king, Saul, who had some promise under the leadership of David and Solomon, then lost their way under the leadership of subsequent kings who were mostly idolaters and unfaithful to God. The Davidic Kingdom was rent in two, Israel to the North, and Judah to the South.

The continued unfaithfulness of both kingdoms brought the theocratic system from a God-led state to a man-led state, which presumed to be theocratic. Israel fell first, conquered by the Assyrian Empire, their cultural identity lost as they were assimilated into the Empire. Judah fell a century later, to the Babylonian Empire, but this time kept their cultural and religious identity intact, carrying the legacy of the Davidic Kingdom into exile.

Suffering the loss of their autonomy, the Jews eventually returned to Jerusalem but as they were still a vassal of the Persian Empire, they longed for the day they could regain their self-governance again. They had a brief respite after the successful Maccabean revolt against their Seleucid overlords gave them relative autonomy but were again under foreign dominion when the Roman Empire claimed the Judean province as part of their Empire.

It was under this context that Jesus Christ, the Son of God was incarnated into human flesh and walked among men. This was the Messiah, but Judah did not recognize its Savior, as they looked for a revolutionary leader that could galvanize the Judean population against their Roman conquerors and set them free just like the Maccabeans did against the Seleucids a century and a half earlier. Instead, they saw a meek and lowly Man, who had thousands follow Him, healed them physically and spiritually, and preached a radical message of a heavenly Kingdom, not built with human hands.

Betrayed by His own, the Messiah was led like a Lamb to the slaughter. But before He was nailed to a wooden cross, He had the opportunity to reveal His true agenda. He had no earthly political ambitions and declared to the Roman governor before Him that His Kingdom is "not of this world". His jurisdiction was way above that which Rome could ever hope to reach, even if they had conquered every inch of the planet.

There is a difference between the sphere which is properly moral, and that sphere that determines that which is properly civil. Because there is a different remedy needed for moral sins than civil crimes, there is a need to separate the two into different spheres of government. This is why American Christian attempts to eliminate the separation of Church and State must be resisted at all costs. When Christ rebuked the crowd that clamored to stone the woman caught in adultery, He admonished them with the realization that they were in no position to execute judgement upon the woman. Whether the punishment for moral sins and heretical deviances be as extreme as stoning and burning at the stake or as light as a mere fine, to execute such a sentence, the judge, jury and executioner must be sinlessly *perfect.* No worldly judge, jury and executioner meets this criterion. All have sinned and fallen short of the glory of God. Therefore, the "powers that be" can only be expected to keep the civil peace among men, using the Jefferson litmus test and punishing civil crimes appropriately, and as best as worldly justice can provide.

The sooner we understand these basic concepts, overcome our tendency to fall into HPRS and remember the harsh lessons of history, the sooner we can work towards a society that is free for all consciences, giving believers and unbelievers alike liberty to freely exercise their right of religious practice, so long as they do not "break a leg" or "pick a pocket". The strength of America is not in a forced conformity to one belief or another, but rather in its "unity in diversity", diverse in race, cultural origin, traditions and religious belief, but united as a nation. There should be freedom for all. Especially in religious belief and non-belief, whether it be for the Christian, Muslim, Hindu, Jew, Buddhist, Wiccan, or the atheist. This is what makes America the greatest nation on Earth. To suggest otherwise would be, frankly, un-American, *and* un-Christian, for while Christians respect and honor their Earthly nation in its sphere, they understand that Christ's Kingdom is, *not of this world.*

About the Author

Lemuel Valendez Sapian was born and raised in Denton, Texas, and holds a Bachelor of Arts degree in History from the University of North Texas. Married with four fast-growing children, his passion is for world, religious, American, and military historical studies. A lifelong Christian, he is an aspiring minister, a business owner, and an avid traveler. He also writes and composes songs and shares his love for music on the guitar and piano.

www.notofthisworldbook.com